POETS

BETWEEN THE WARS

A NEW CANADIAN LIBRARY ORIGINAL NO. 05

M&S

POETS

BETWEEN THE WARS

E. J. Pratt F. R. Scott A. J. M. Smith Dorothy Livesay A. M. Klein

EDITED AND WITH AN INTRODUCTION BY Milton Wilson

GENERAL EDITOR: Malcolm Ross

Canadian Cataloguing in Publication Data

Main entry under title:
Poets between the wars

(New Canadian library; no. 05)
ISBN 0-7710-9475-2

1. Canadian poetry (English) – 20th century.*
I. Pratt, E.J. (Edwin John), 1882-1964.
II. Wilson, Milton, 1923-   . III. Series.

PS8291.P64 1989   C811'.52'08   C89-094045-2
PR9195.7.P64 1989

Manufactured in Canada by Webcom Limited

McClelland & Stewart Inc.
The Canadian Publishers
481 University Avenue
Toronto, Ontario
M5G 2E9

Contents

INTRODUCTION

The five poets of this anthology came to maturity between the First and Second World Wars, but all of them continued to write, not only after 1939, but after 1945, and all but one are still living today. The poems which I have chosen range from their earlier to their more recent work. In other words, this is not a period anthology with 1918 and 1939 as its outer limits, but a generation anthology, and the generation of poets is the one which emerged unmistakably and chalked up its first notable achievements in the twenties and thirties, and which has been trying to maintain or improve on those achievements ever since. The pages which follow this brief introduction offer not the poetry between the wars, but rather the poets – which turns out to be a far more comprehensive thing.

Poets between the Wars is based on the same general assumption as its predecessors in this series, *Poets of the Confederation* and *Poetry of Mid-Century*, namely, that there is a place, particularly on the Canadian scene, for the kind of anthology that chooses a very few poets and gives them as many pages as possible, rather than the kind that chooses as many poets as possible and gives them a few pages each. The choice of E. J. Pratt for inclusion makes that assumption especially appropriate. Because it is possible to devote nearly eighty pages to his work, three narrative poems can be printed in full, including two of his longest. Thus the Canadian poet least amenable to anthologies is at his most amenable here.

Such are the principles and scope of this anthology. Their exemplification is a more questionable matter. While the choice of these five poets—Pratt, Smith, Scott, Klein, and Livesay—strikes me as almost inescapable, the choice of particular poems certainly is not. But to defend his taste or to advertise his wares is not the anthologist's business. A collection like this is self-justifying if it is justifiable at all.

MILTON WILSON

Trinity College,
University of Toronto

E. J. PRATT

The son of a Methodist minister, E. J. Pratt was born in the small Newfoundland village of Western Bay in 1883 and received his early education at Methodist College, St. John's. He spent four years working in Newfoundland villages, first as a schoolteacher and then as a probationer for the Methodist ministry, before leaving the island and attending Victoria College in the University of Toronto, from which he graduated with a B.A. in 1911. Although his graduate work was in psychology and theology, and he wrote theses on demonology and Pauline eschatology, he nevertheless, after receiving a B.D. in 1913 and a PH.D. in 1917, joined the English Department of Victoria College in 1919, and he taught there until his retirement in 1953. He was gregarious, hospitable, and blessed with an immense fund of anecdotes, and no one who met him during these thirty years can have found him easy to forget. *Newfoundland Verse* was published in 1923 and *The Witches' Brew* in 1925. After the critical and popular success of the two long narrative poems ("The Cachalot" and "The Great Feud") which make up *Titans* (1926), his reputation in Canada established itself in a succession of books, all, like the earlier ones, published by Macmillan: *The Iron Door* (1928), *The Roosevelt and the Antinoe* (1930), *Verses of the Sea* (1930), *Many Moods* (1932), *The Titanic* (1946), *The Fable of the Goats and Other Verse* (1937), *Brébeuf and His Brethren* (1940), *Dunkirk* (1941), *Still Life and Other Verse* (1943), *They Are Returning* (1946), *Behind the Log* (1947), and *Towards the Last Spike* (1952). A *Collected Poems* was published in 1944 and in 1958. Except for a brief flurry of American interest in the early forties, Pratt has not made much impression beyond the borders of Canada; his unfashionable kind of originality has resisted export, and no country is likely to adopt another's culture hero. But for Canadian readers he has become the one inescapable, large-scale figure in their poetic history. He died in 1964.

The Great Feud

(A Dream of a Pleiocene Armageddon)

Like a quarter moon the shoreline curled
Upon the neck of the ancient world,
Where, as the modern Magians say,
In one cool morning of the Earth,
Australasia had its birth,
And vertebrated with Malay.
Monsoons from Arafura Seas
Had played their native energies
Full upon the western tip,
Until the vast recessional
Of scourging wash and tidal rip
Had made a stubborn littoral
Take on a deep indented shape,–
A hundred leagues, to the eastern Cape,
Of broken bays with narrow reaches,
Deltas and gulfs bulwarked by steep
Eroded headlands, with a sweep
Of fifty miles of central beaches,
And rich alluvial flats where luscious
Grasses, ferns and milk bulrushes
Made up the original nursery
For fauna of the land and sea.

Stretching from the water line
By gentle slope and sharp incline,
Past many an undulating plain,
The land ran southward to a chain
Of heavy-wooded hills and rose
Beyond them to the Black Sierras,
Soaring aloft to where the snows
That capped the ranging Guadeleras
Were blackened by the brooding dread
Outline of a volcano's head, –
Jurania, with her crater jaw,
Her slanting forehead ancient-scarred,
And breathing through her smoky maw,
Lay like a dragon left to guard
The Isthmian Scarps against the climb
Of life that left the ocean slime,
In far adventurous design,
On footholds past the timber line.
In such a place, at such a time,
Long before the birth of man,
This great Tellurian feud began.

For ages which cannot be told
The fish along the Isthmian border
Had felt the invasion of their cold
Blood by an unexplained disorder.
It looked as if the destination,
Of all life of the stock marine,
Was doomed to be, through paths unseen,
The most profound obliteration.
Millions of youthful fins were led
Far from their safe and watery bed,
To sport along the tidal edge,
Nosing for grubs and water-lice,
For pickerel weed and shoots of rice
That grew luxuriant within the sedge,
And many feasting unawares
Were drawn into relentless snares;
Strange rasp-and-saw bills harried them,
And swooping talons carried them
Into the air, and many more
Were stranded high and dry on shore,
Where poisonous lizards, asps and adders
Bit them, or where the solar fire

Caught them at noon-tide in the mire,
Curdled their blood and starched their bladders.
And thousands that survived the heat
Turned their backs upon their breed,
Shed their fins and took on feet,
And clambered far inland to feed
On windy things like grass and roots,
Bark and leaves and bitter sloes,
Or, like those horrid jungle brutes
With hairy pelts and horny toes,
To quaff the warm blood of their foes;
While many more that did return,
After one æonian night,
Came back contemptuous to spurn
Their parents, like the trilobite,
With stony back and stonier heart;
Rolled up in balls and dwelt apart
In sulky isolation; while others, –
The mongrel water scorpions sprung
From crabs and spiders, – came and stung
Their little sisters and their brothers.

And thus it was throughout the whole
Sea-range of the Australian zone,
The fear of racial doom was thrown
Heavily upon the piscine soul.
A futile anger like a curse
Only made confusion worse.
Their mad desire to strike back
At their destroying coward-foe
Turned all their fury of attack
Into consuming vertigo.
It broke their hearts and crushed their wills,
It thinned the juices of their maws,
Left them with gnashing of the jaws
And deep prolapsis of the gills.
And hitherto unsuffered pains,
A ghastly brood, came in by legions,
Rheumatic tremors in the veins,
And palsy in the ventral regions.
Now, not a single evening passed
But an aquatic breathed its last
Beneath the terrifying roar

Of some dread plantigrade on shore;
And so this strange insidious spark
Of wild adventure carried sorrow
To many a yearning matriarch
With the drab dawning of the morrow.
But worst of all the horrors which
Enmeshed them was the galling sense
That never would the recompense
Of battle come; that primal itch
For vengeance would expend its force,
According to an adverse Fate,
Running a self-destroying course
Down the blind alley of their hate.
But by some quirk that Nature flings
Into the settled scheme of things, –
That old beldame, she gets so grumpy,
No mortal vision may foretell
Her antics, when her nerves are jumpy –
It happened that she broke the spell
By a freak shifting of the odds
Within the sea-lap of the gods.

Vibrant calms unknown before
Lay on the Australasian shore,
And Silences, a hooded band,
Like portents of catastrophe,
Tip-toed expectant on the land,
And mummed about the open sea.
Neptune had resigned the trident,
For months Aeolus had not spoken,
Nor had the sea-waves heard the strident
Trumpeter, – his conch was broken.
From igneous fissures in the ground
Blue wisps of smoke with eerie sound
Curled on the air to indicate
That some elaborate escapade
Was on the point of being played
By the royal clowns of Fate.
Here and there through asphalt holes
Was heard a most uncanny racket, –
Charon, before the birth of souls
Called for his modern Stygian packet,
Was busy at enormous scows,
Caulking them with walrus skin,

Hammering, sawing to the din
Of Cerberus with his gruff bow-wows,
Together with the gird and clatter
Of wheels and whiffletrees, the croak
Of scranny throats, and the fast patter
Of feet and flap of wings, that spoke
Of straining, jostling ambulances;
Of Hecate with a frightful brood
Of harpies in a phantom wood,
Rehearsing new macabre dances.
Now all this strange activity
Was radiating everywhere;
It rapped the calms upon the sea,
It shot through flumes of stagnant air,
It tingled in the blood of brutes
Of land and water; in the roots
Of trees; and even stuff like rocks
Felt the strong etheric shocks,
Until all natural things that dwelt
In the marine Australian belt
Had come to feel, in a dumb way,
That their protracted evil spell
Might, with the birth of any day,
Dissolve before a miracle.

One vital morning when the tide
Was out and the Scala flats were dried,
The largest-livered, heaviest-brained,
Most thoroughbred pedestrian
Of all the tribes that had attained
The rank of the amphibian,
A green-back turtle left the sea.
Her blood was changing and a scent,
Unknown to her rude ancestry,
Had charged her with presentiment
Of some unfathomed destiny.
She had her eyes upon a spot
She long aspired to, but had not
For lack of muscle, wind and time,
Been able to effect the climb.
To-day, with fast evolving legs,
Urged by the lure of distant land,
She struggled for this cone of sand,
Proudly there to lay her eggs,

And from this vantage point, some day,
To take her young and wend her way,
Far up into the hills, to view
What kind of giant there might dwell
Stretched asleep against the blue,–
A turtle with a snow-white shell,
Or inland whale, for aught she knew,
Sending through a spiracle,
Intermittent puffs of grey
Cloud resembling ocean spray.
But when after four dusty hours
She reached the top of the sandy cone,
A thrill her blood had never known
Paralysed her laying powers,
And concentrated all her thought
Upon the scene the morning brought.

An amphitheatre that held
Valleys and cliffs and waterfalls,
Gorges hewn like royal halls,
Forests flanked by hills that swelled
To mountains, these again to clouds
From peaks of ice; and everywhere
On ground, in trees and in the air,
All forms of living things; dense crowds
Of kites and gulls; vultures that hung
Within the blue; and mangabees;
Pig-tailed baboons that peered and swung
From the liana of the trees;
Wombats beneath acacias;
Tasmanian tigers in the grass;
Civets and sloths and bandicoots;
High-standing elks in hollowed stumps
Of redwood; tapirs in the clumps
Of banyan, grubbing at the roots;
And under eucalyptus trees,
Flocks of emus and kiwis,
With herds of skipping kangaroos,
Antelopes and brindled gnoos;–
All Earth's delegates were sent,
Blood relations, tribal foes,
Bound by cordial entente,
To this prodigious Parliament;–
Lions and water-buffaloes,

Clouded leopards, chamois droves,
Side by side and cheek by nose,
Rested in the myrtle groves;
While pumas, rams and grizzly bears
Stroked each other in their lairs.
And central to this wild tableau,
A white giraffe began to scale
A scraggy monolith of shale,
Standing on a high plateau.
And when his neck had arched the summit,
A female anthropoidal ape
Climbed up, and settling on the nape,
Surveyed the crowded congress from it.
The comeliest of the Primate race,
No one of all the Southern lands
Could match her for arboreal grace,
For hairy contour of her hands,
For contemplation in her face,
Or wisdom in her thyroid glands.
To hide her young, to fight or climb,
She was the cleverest of her time.
She taught the family tribes to make
A brier or a bamboo stake,
Fashion an eolith and throw
It deadly at a distant foe,
To charge in serried ranks, or beat
A hurried or prepared retreat,
Showed them new uses for their paws
In battle for the monkey cause.
And faintly she had sniffed the raw
Material of the moral law;
She had observed, one windy night,
The skull of an alligator cut
Open by a cocoanut
Falling from a lofty height, –
An alligator that had torn
And eaten up her youngest born.
Then to a corner she had crept,
And had not eaten, had not slept,
But scratched her head and drummed her breast,
And Reason entered as she wondered,
Brooded in the trees and pondered
On how the reptile was struck dead.
And now on wide and just behalf

Of all the land brutes of the world,
She took the leadership and curled
Around the neck of the giraffe;
And all at once confusion ceased,
As every hard raptorial beak
And slanted eye of bird and beast
Were strained upon the central peak, –
And every lobe of every ear
Was cocked that none might fail to hear
The message when the ape unfurled
Her simian marvel to the world.

All ye that dwell afar or nigh
Upon the plains or on the hills,
In valley caves or in the sky,
Feathers, and bristles, talons, quills,
Flesh-eating ones and herbivores
That roam inland or ramp the shores;
All ye with snouts that turn the furrow
For colonies of ants or burrow
For savoury roots and fattened worms;
And ye that carry on your sides
Impenetrable armour hides,
Slow-moving; ponderous pachyderms;
All ye that lie in wait and crouch
And gnashing leap upon your prey;
And those that at the breast or pouch
Suckle the young; all ye that lay,
And scratch the ant-hills with your claws;
And all that brotherhood that climb,
Cracking great nuts between the jaws;
Give ear and know ye that the time
Has come when he that slumbereth
Shall pay the penalty of death.

Turn ye your gaze, a moment, far
Beyond the plain over the height
Of the palm trees where the white
Foam-line breaks upon the bar.
There under the blue stretch of sea,
Living in darkness out of sight
Skulks our ancient enemy,
Devouring everything that passes
Along the great lagoons to feed

On clams and shrimps and rich swamp grasses
Growing beside the tidal weed.
By right of conquest and of birth
We claim all footholds on this Earth;—
Those flats there steaming in the sun,
The coast-line to the salted edge
Where the coral foam is spun,
That long three-cornered, rocky wedge
On which the walrus warms his hide,
Where the dugong sleeps,—which the manatee
Claims as his dwelling when the sea
Sucks it from us at high tide.
All ye that hail from foreign parts
Whose warm blood knocking at your hearts
Has led you to this southern place,
Attend upon my words! and know
What great disaster to our race
Befell us thirty years ago.
You noticed as you cleared the height
Of the Aral range that, to the south,
Three juts of land came into sight,
Extending far out of the mouth
Of the Ravenna river;—these
Have ever been the nurseries
For the monkey tribe and kangaroo,
For gentle bears and wallabies,
For marmoset and wanderoo,
And for the crinkly-tail baboon.
On one dread summer day—at noon—
A terror broke upon our eyes;
We saw the blazing sun go out,
And the level sea begin to rise
Under the breath of a typhoon,
And break with tidal water-spout,
Carrying with the general ruin
Of the palms, the aged and the young,
The mother bear and little bruin;
And wailing mandrill babes that clung
To the parental neck were flung
Into the watery abyss
To satisfy the avarice
And lust of every carrion foe
And devil-fish that dwelt therein.
To-day that slaughter at the Delta

Remains the nightmare of the years;
Those death-cries of the apes could melt a
Stony crocodile to tears.
Since then, their blood-thirst unappeased,
They've ventured up our quiet streams;
Gannets and herons have been seized,
Baboons have died with horrid screams,
And elephantine calves for miles
All along the water-courses,
Together with young water-horses,
Have been dragged down by crocodiles.
For years reports have been received
From distant countries occupied
By furs, feathers and hairs allied
By blood, how they have been bereaved
And plunged in blackest misery
By that insane, consuming hate
Of ignorant, inarticulate,
Cold-blood barbarians of the sea.
All we observant ones have seen
That at high tides in clouded moons
The habits of the fish have been
To pass into the great lagoons,
To lie in wait throughout the course
Of night and morning to midday,
Then chase our swimming breeds and slay
Them with no feeling of remorse;
And then with foul-distended maw,
The cowards that they are withdraw
To their unlighted haunts, to shun
An open struggle in the sun.
Therefore, let it now be known,
By tokens that can never err, –
By the marrow in the fox's bone,
By the light growth of the ermine's fur,
And by the camel's drinking bout,
That the season's blasting drought,
With lowering of the tides, will last
Till three up-tilted moons have passed.
Then will the inland shallows be
At all their gateways unexposed
To the waters of the open sea,
When the barrier reefs have closed.
So if our hearts are resolute,

At the appointed hour we'll match them
With our brave hosts in massed pursuit;
No quarter shall there be: we'll catch them,—
From the smallest to the largest brute—
Throw them into consternation,
Hem them in the muddy places
And on the shoals, leaving no traces
Save of their damned annihilation.
Before I close—just one word more.
Oft have we seen a jealous raid
Grow into a great crusade;
Or end by internecine war,
When the blood of kindred drenched
The higher mountain snows and quenched
The jungle grass and arid moors.
Therefore ye thirsty carnivores
Be ye adjured that till the hour
Of trial ye shall not devour
The flesh of either animal
Or bird upon the Earth; nor shall
Ye taste of blood; your daily food
Shall be the Earth's fair yield of fruits,
Her store of plants and sappy roots,
The fresh rind of the sandalwood,
And willow bark, berries and beans,
Tussac grass and mangosteens,
Papaws and guavas and the sweet
Milk of the cocoanut, the meat
Of durian with celery,
The ripe fruit of the mango-tree;
Yea—all the natural plentitude
Of Earth shall henceforth be your food.
Likewise ye herbivores, be ye
Adjured against all enmity.
Ye shall not trample; shall not gore,
With hoof or horn, the carnivore;
But as their allies, ye shall spend,
In one grand consummating blow
Of death against the common foe,
Your strength to a triumphant end.
Now hie ye to your lairs; sleep not;
Gather your hosts; abate no jot
Of this day's wrath, and when the year
Is big with three up-tilted moons,

We'll charge on the aquatics here,
And trap them in the great Lagoons.

She spoke: and every throat and lung
Of herbivore and carnivore,
In volleying symphonic roar,
Rang with persuasion of her tongue.
With vengeance firing, up the breast,
And with the speed of a monsoon blast,
The keen dispersing hordes soon passed
Beyond the skyline of the West.
And the sultriness of peace again
Brooded on valley, hill and plain,
Shaken only when a cloud
Of thick Juranian vapour, thrown
In a dark spiral, burst with loud
Echoes, like laughter from the cone.

Scrambling from her hill of sand,
The disillusioned, now unfertile,
Amphibious and bilingual turtle
Fled the spectre of the land;
Crossed the muddy flats and sought her
Endangered kindred of the water,
Apprised them of their bloody fate;
The congress vote; the rage and hate
Of the ape; her story of the feud,
And the news was borne at ether rate
Throughout the ocean's amplitude,
And hailed with fierce, exultant mood,
With wave of pectorals and high leap
Into the air and foamy sweep
Of tail and clutch of tentacle;
Broken was the hoary spell!
The hour for revenge, for daring,
Had come for fin and scale and shell!
For shark! swordfish! mackerel!
Lobster! octopus! and herring!

(With the Passage of the Moons)

THE MUSTER

Black bucks whose distant ancestry
Sprang from the (now) Westphalian hills;
Wild boars with hair as stiff as quills,
Or Brandenburgian pedigree;
Wallachian elks, whose antlers spread
A full five feet above the head,
Trekked around the Caucasus,
Sounding with defiant stare
Their gutturals blent with blasphemous
Umlauts upon the stricken air;
And they were joined near Teheran
By camels down from Turkestan,
And elands from Trans-Caspian snows,
Persian gazelles with harts and roes,
Arabian antelopes and masses
Of quaggas, zebras and wild asses;
And on the eastern move, they met
Horses following in the tracks
Of ibexes and shaggy yaks
From South Bokhara and Thibet
And countries far-distributed;
The thunderous Indian quadruped,–
Rhinoceros and elephant,
And every kind of ruminant,
And non-cud-chewing animals,
Mammal and marsupial;
From hill and valley, steppe and prairie,
Peccary and dromedary,
Bashan bull and Cashmir ram,
The male spring-bok, chamois, gnoo,
The reid-buck and the kangaroo
Heading downwards through Siam.
Likewise, with earth-shattering roars,
Accompanied by the screams of birds,
From the wide compass came the herds
Of storming, hungry carnivores.
On them the patriotic call
Fell with the greatest sacrifice.
A troop of tigers from Bengal,
Full of caraway and rice,

(In keeping with the simian pledge)
Discovering early that their edge
Of appetite was dulled enough
By such ill-regulated stuff
Upon a base of hops and oats,
Attacked (although they did not slay)
A flock of Himalayan goats
Resting on a wooded height
In their mid-journey to Malay;
They drained their udders, bleached them white,
And leaving them in awful plight,
Prostrate and helpless for the fray,
Passed on with energy renewed
Into the Australasian feud.
Through scorching plains and bleak defiles
Of Northern India's spacious miles,
Spread a vast host of tawny, mad
Lions from Allahabad.
Oleanders, roots of taro
With ginseng and dried kauri cones
Had changed the substance of their marrow,
And alternated growls with groans.
Hyænas forced-fed on salt-bush
With sago palms and tapioca
Wailed so loudly that they woke a
Pack of wolves from Hindu Kush,
Whose tocsin cry antiphonal
Was caught by every caracal
Sleeping with his stomach full
Of rhododendrons near Cabul;
And this was followed by the blab
Of jackals cursed with elderberry
All the way from the Punjab
As far South-East as Pondicherry.
Over the stretch from Turkestan,
From Shamo Desert to Hunan,
From Shantung down to Singapore,
Along the central isthmus, fell
The mighty, myrmidonian roar,
That ululant and choric yell
Of leopards full of okra pods
And lentils; cheetahs gagging hard
At cascarilla spiced with nard;
Polecats charged with cotton wads,

And bears and civets overcome
With stringent eucalyptus gum.
All these in thousands numberless
Had, with the triple lunar round,
Arrived, in hot blood-thirstiness,
Upon the Isthmian battle ground,
Where, when the welter of their roars
Had ceased along the littoral border,
The hordes were disciplined to order,
Divided into army corps,
Brigades, battalions and platoons;
Some were ambushed by the coast
In heavy scrub and bush, but most
Were stationed near the great lagoons
Connected with the hostile beaches,
And regimented into shape
By the anthropoidal ape
Who, by her rousing martial speeches,
Kept up to fever heat their zeal
For the imperilled commonweal.
At last when the appointed week
Had come; and when the final night
Was over with the first faint streak
Of orange in the Eastern light, —
Just at the hour when every pad
And hoof were tingling with the mad
Moment of impending slaughter,
A reeking, ghastly, unknown flair
Compounded of the earth and water,
Of subterranean clay and air,
And like no other scent, arose
And fell upon each roving nose.

Over the top of the nearest alp
A cliff-like head began to rise;
A lizard's skull with horny scalp,
Dragon's teeth and boa's eyes;
Covered with scales of greenish blue
The lower jaw swung into view,
And from the open mouth there came
A lolling tongue of scarlet flame;
A column of a neck whose reach
Topped the high branches of a beech;
Prehensile arms and girthy paunch

Upheld by massive spine and haunch
Are followed by unmeasured thighs;
With hock and joint the inches rise,
Until the monster in dread sight
Of all, to the last claw, collects
His stature on the Aral height,
And lo,–TYRANNOSAUROS REX!

Now let the sceptic disbelieve
The truth I am about to state,
And urge, with curling lip, I weave
A legend that is out of date.
Let him disgorge his lie; I claim
That by a wanton twist of Fate,
(To which I am by Hera sworn)
A creature of this sounding name,
Although three millions years too late,
Stood on that peak this awful morn.
It came to pass, one day, before
Mammals appeared upon the Earth,
A dinosaurian mother bore
Tyrannus in a tragic birth.
Chasing a mighty stegosaur
Into a bed of pitch, she tried,
With huge success, before she died,
To lay an egg that chanced to live
Throughout its long bituminous night,
Enveloped by this soft, air-tight
Most excellent preservative;
Until just fifty years ago,
When the volcano underwent
Her seismal periodic throe,
The egg came bouncing through a rent.
A moa passing by espied
The object; sidled up, cock-eyed,
And watched it with a mother's pride.
Like a beach-stone pumiced by the sea,
It glowed with the full sunlight on it.
She sniffed the thing excitedly,
Walked around it, pecked and scratched
The shell, then feathered down upon it.
And in due course of time she hatched
Her prodigy. At first she fed him
On cotton-tails and unweaned lambs,

On calves and badgers; then she led him
To the higher ridges where she filled
His stomach with the coarser hams
Of pigs and short-horn mountain rams,
Until he took on strength and killed
All comers with their sires and dams.

Now after fifty years, the bird
Had, from a cassowary, heard
About the Pan-cyclonic rally
Of beasts in the Juranian Valley,
And how at their great gastric session
They swore to stand by the Food Concession.
And so the moa felt she'd serve her
Race the best, fanning the wild
Instinct of her foster child
With her strong patriotic fervour.
She found *this* lesson easy for
A huge blood-quaffing dinosaur;
The next one that she strove to teach, –
To feed on rushes, roots and grass, –
Seemed to this hungry ward, alas,
Beyond his intellectual reach.
Still, after days of bleats and pants,
Of clucking at the balsam cones,
Of digging graves for flesh and bones,
And building pyramids of plants; –
And after days of petulant scolding,
She managed to convey, by holding
Within her talons, cocoanuts
And bread-fruit rather than the cuts
From the sirloin of putrid cattle, –
That fasting from all flesh and blood,
And chewing, self-imposed, of cud,
Was the condition of the battle.
And so the fatal morning found
Him bloated, angry and unsound
Of wind and reeling down the height
For flesh, his object of the fight.
His skyward neck took on the form
Of a pliant topmast in a storm.
His headlong and unsteady gait
Had been the more provoked, of late,
By a yeasty alimentary state.

For, on the day before, twitch grass
With coarse buck wheat and sassafras
Had formed the staple of his diet.
A vinery of red grape then lay
Before him; he resolved to try it;
Which done, his head began to sway,
The hot, fermenting liquor rose,
And just before the charge was made,
Had sluiced up through his neck, and played
A geyser through his throat and nose,
Until his body seemed to seethe
With dragon foam on scale and claw,
The scarlet dripping from his teeth,
And fire issuing from his jaw.
The ape had feared the monster's coming
Would cause a panic as the sound
Of thunder from the infernal drumming
Of Tyrannus' feet upon the ground,
Breaking like waves along the coast,
Fell upon the affrighted host.
And for a moment as he neared
The rostral monolith and tossed
His head for carnage it appeared
As if the national cause was lost.
So strong the impact as he hit
A line of tigers near the centre
It paralysed the simian's wit
And for a fearful second rent her
Courage as the jungle mass
Went floundering in a deep morass.
But instant as a thunderclap
The prescience of her soul awoke,
For by that self-same tiger stroke
Tyrannosauros filled the gap,
And as the stress upon the line
Was centrally towards the sea,
She caught the panic's energy
Of flight in time, and flashed the sign
Of battle from her lofty tower,
Then launched the seething frenzied power
Of tusk and claw. Blood red the Dawn!
The die was cast! The fight was on!

Now was seen the strategy
Hidden in the stern decree
Of the wise old anthropoid.
The long-continued carnal void,
With all its gastric irritation,
Had raised their lust to slay and eat
Raw flesh to the internal heat
Of a universal conflagration.
Just in from dry Allahabad,
Farinaceous lions had
Spied, upon an oozy bank,
Five hundred head of walruses,
Their hides of rubber steaming rank
With odours oleaginous.
Such was their fury when they smelled them,
It seemed as if the nether air
Were raining tails and brindled hair, –
The way those brutes of India felled them;
They had them stripped before the sun
Arose to bleach each skeleton.
Fifteen miles farther down the Coast,
An angry and conglomerate host, –
Inflammatory Bengalese,
Starved with cherry bark and peas;
With salicaceous jaguars,
Leguminous leopards full of beans
That murmured in their jugulars, –
Swooped, with the speed of peregrines,
Upon the red substantial meals
Of dolphins hot and blubberous,
And a large school of porpoises,
Manatees and ursine seals,
Until the sand-spit where they were
Surrendered back unto the sea
Not one shred of fat or fur
But polished skulls and vertebrae.
Down a sharp declivity
Where the eastern skyline touched a plain,
Wild cats of Burmese demonry
Fell like a cloud of typhoon rain.
Raisins had so alkalized them
That the fur upon their necks had moulted,
Soyas and poppies which they bolted
Stuck in their throats and agonized them.

So swift and vital was their spring
When circling round a "Sulphur Bottom",
They drove him on the rocks and got 'im
Like turkey buzzards on the wing,
Pouncing on a carrion,
Until beneath the morning sky
His ribs were arching high and dry
Like the frame of a stranded galleon.

With the first hours of the day
It seemed the battle fortunes lay
In ample margins with the land.
No courage of the sea could stand
Against the all-consuming, savage
Hunger springing from such a fast,
Nor millions numberless outlast
That crash of pyramidal ravage.
But with the pangs of thirst abated,
A temporary slackening of the drive
Gave to the fish infuriated
With loss a moment to revive
Their ranks, when soon upon the air
New cries of terror and despair
Announced destruction for the land.
Rounding the Roc peninsula,
Sperm whales from Carpentaria
Had reached the Dura bank of sand,
And bellying round, began to blow
Their challenge in contemptuous spout
At any brute the earth could show
Possessing horn or tusk or snout.
Undaunted, a battalion
Of bulling elephants from Canton,
Directed by a jackass, tore
Their ponderous course down to the shore,
In answer to the loud defiance
Of those humpbacked mammalian giants.
Lured by the low ebb of the tide,
And a hundred yards of bar, sun-dried,
They plunged into the quicksands where,
With roar of suction and the blare
Of strained uplifted trunks, they died,
Or slipping into weedy ground
Off the silting edge, were drowned

At leisure by the sweeping tails
And jaw-tug of victorious whales.

Down at the delta of Ravenna,
The hardest struggle of the day
For three long hours was under way,
Wild as the tumult of Gehenna.
A thousand tigers of the land
Were fighting, under the command
Of a Sumatran chimpanzee,
Ten thousand tigers of the sea.
The thirstier cats that formed the van
Took the water, swimming far
Beyond the shallows of the bar,
Heedless of the risk they ran;
Others of more tempered daring,
Striking the water margin, kept
Well within their depth but swept
Along the muddy regions, tearing
The placid surface into spray,
Like a gale's lash upon a bay.
For those three hours the waters ran
With every hue of the rainbow span, –
Saffron lines and serpentine,
Lurid darts of iris green,
Mottled browns with dusky stripe,
Eyeballs flashing streaks of red,
Leaped and zigzagged to the gripe
Of lamia and of hammerhead,
Locking with inveterate teeth
The tigers' bellies underneath.
Phantoms blue and ashen pale
Followed white ones in the race
Where blade of dorsal, scythe of tail
Cut and ripped the water's face,
Curved and sank while in their place
The vitreous glare of stomachs rose
With flapping pectorals, as the claws
Of tigers tore a bottle-nose
Or bullet-head; or as their jaws,
Just at the moment they were drowned,
With paralysing seizure found
Their last authentic tiger mark
In the marble throat of a slate-blue shark.

And when the fierce dispute was over,
And the tides were crimson in the sun,
The splash of a ground shark or the dun
Lithe shadow of an ocean rover,
Cutting across the backward spins
Of settling eddies showed how vast
Was the jungle ruin when at last
The furs were conquered by the fins.

Beyond the edge of the chalk canal,
In the deeper part of the Skibo Run
The tiger slaughter was outdone
By a longer, bloodier carnival.
There, neutral hippopotami,
Spotted deer, mild-mannered sows,
Milk-white mules and buffalo cows
Had wandered with their young to lie
And bathe beneath a peaceful sky,
With antelopes and quagga mares,
Soft gazelles and brown she-bears,
Frightened by the roars that rent
The rafters of the firmament;
When suddenly as by design
It seemed as if the whole Pacific
Had yielded up her most terrific
Monsters of the fighting line.
Their long blades flashing in the sun,
Sword-fish were swimming up the Run,
Accompanied by flagitious things,—
Saw-bills with their deadly pikes,
Thornbacks with their poisoned spikes,
Torpedo rays with scorpion stings;
Most feared by everything that lives
Above the ocean floor, they broke
With full mortality of stroke
On neutrals and on fugitives,
Hemmed them backwards from the beaches
Into the water's deeper reaches,
Where with rapiers lightning sped,
They took the measure of their sides,
Till all the antelopes were dead,
And all the hippos' leathery hides
Transfixed and all the bears were drilled
With holes and all the calves were killed.

Now late within the afternoon
Again the tide of battle changed.
Fish from the Seven Seas were ranged
Along the stretch of the Blue Lagoon
That had beneath the withering spell
Of three hot rainless moons been closed.
There, lash-rays – the marines of hell –
Had come with sharks, – the shovel-nosed,
And sickle-finned; dog-fish, big jacks
Gifted with prophetic smell, –
All following in the conquering tracks
Of threshers from the Hebrides,
Of Greenland killers and those mailed,
Tremendous rhinodons that hailed
From the typhoons of the Indian seas.
Against that swarming, heaving pack
Was launched the raving, massed attack
Of full-grown argali, and rams
From South Afghanistan that mourned
The swordfish slaughter of their dams;
And fighting boars that would have scorned
Brigades of tigers, with koodoos,
Flanked by battalions of gnoos,
And bull-head rhinos double-horned.
Into that reeling, shapeless ruck,
Scarce covered by the water, poured
This furious and avenging horde. . . .
Surviving rhinodons that struck
For ocean spaces through the ford
Were caught fast in the mire, and gored
To death by stag and water-buck.

And as the dubious hours went by,
Cormorants, in carrion mood,
Ospreys and kestrels thronged the sky,
Impatient, as the fiery feud
Swung through such vicissitude
As never, after or before,
Was known within the files of War.
Such acts of valour as were done
Outshone the white flame of the sun; –
Such hopeless sacrificial deeds
And feats of strength as might belong
To men or gods, when weaker breeds

Wrecked their bodies on the strong.
Reversals with the strangest luck,
Unknown to contests in the sea,
Took place where bulk and energy
Matched themselves with skill and pluck.
Mackerel and electric eels
Drowned zebras, weighting down their thighs;
Leonine and ursine seals
Were killed by lemurs and aye-ayes.
To rescue otters with their young
From saw-fish and an instant slaughter,
A scouting beaver party flung
Themselves into the salted water,
Were caught, outnumbered and were beaten,
Run through by bayonet-bills, and eaten.
But their assailants blown with greed
Were seized, after the hottest chase,
By hounds of an Eo-Irish race,
And terriers of a Gallic breed.
And the sun went down upon the sight
Of bison worsted by becunas,
Of foxes putting sharks to flight
And weasels at the throats of tunas.
Along the shore from tip to tip,
This interlocking battle grip
Relaxed only as either side
Gave ground with flow and ebb of tide;
For all were pledged, with teeth and claws,
To racial blood and comradeship,
Devoted to the national cause
And loyal to the boundary strip.

In one swift hour when the night
Was far advanced, the Saurian,
By some half-blinded route, began
To scent the issue of the fight.
Throughout the day he did not know
Which was his ally or his foe;
Beyond the blue lagoon he waded
Where sluggish alligators hid
Behind a sand-spit, and invaded
The rocky strongholds of the squid.
With his steep claws he rent apart
Amphibia along the shore,

And wandering farther out, he tore
Pelagic mammals to the heart.
He followed up a narwhal, wedged
Him dry upon the Gumra shoals,
Left him with twenty streaming holes
From twelve-inch canines double-edged.
Then back upon his tracks he wheeled,
Floundered through the littoral mud,
Entered the battle zone and reeled
Through mounting sloughs of flesh and blood,
Scattering a full hyæna pack
That hung all day upon his track
Along the freshly swollen moors,
Wondering how their nostrils missed
The secret of those bloody spoors
Left by the alien Atavist.
Fish and land animals alike
Were objects for his fangs to strike;
Elephants and jungle cats
Met the same fate as hares and rats;
Beneath his horned, gigantic toes
Camels went down and buffaloes;
And wild cats were so many fleas
That tickled him below the knees.
But when the evening wore to night
Gorillas under cover hit him
With flying stones, and cave bears bit him;
A flock of eagles bleared his sight
With beak and claw; a downy pack
Of monkeys in a sycamore
Swung downward by their tails and tore
The scaly armour from his back.
The bravest lions in the ranks
Buried their teeth into his hocks;
From hemlock crotches and from rocks,
Tigers leaping on his shanks
Gouged deeply with insistent claws
And dropped with flitches in their jaws.
Then from this unremitting stress
Came the sure touch of weariness;
A pulse of apprehension dim
Of what this struggle double-faced
Might in the outcome mean to him.
Perhaps some inland desert taste

During the slaughter of the camels,
Taught him his kinship with the lizard,
His blood-removal from the mammals,
And gave him nausea at the gizzard.
Perhaps in some sharp way it sprang
From the reminiscent tang
Of salt sea water on his muzzle,
The moment that he stooped and took
The narwhal's blood as from a brook
With one inebriating guzzle.
Something in his racial birth,
At variance with the things of Earth,—
A tidal call that beat like pain
From spinal ganglion to brain—
Now made him shake his foes aside,
And leave the battle's desperate zone,
And wander off to climb alone
A promontory where the tide
Sounded its nocturnal flow
A sheer three hundred feet below.
He cleared the base, his body fagged,
And clambered on from shard to shard,
Pausing, jibbing, breathing hard.
Under his weight his knee-caps sagged;
Bleeding fast from fissures torn
By tiger fang and rhino horn,
He groped and stumbled up until
He reached a level granite sill;
Raw fillets hanging from his thighs,
He sank a moment faint with pain;
Chaos was closing on his eyes,
When the voice of the sea-god called again,
Far across the water,—"Ex-
Saurian of the Pleiocene,
Blind wanderer from the race marine,
TYRANNOSAUROS REX!"
Starting sharply from his swoon,
He stood upright, his figure set
Black like a poplar's silhouette
Against the orb of an inflamed moon.
And once again from a crystal bell,
Oceanus wove his spell;
Sounding like a three-fold ring,
Steepled in the crimson surge,

It tolled . . .
"TYRANNOSAUROS!
      TYRANNOSAUROS!
           TYRANNOSAUROS KING!"
The lizard staggered to the verge,
Looked into the water's face,
The rolling cradle of his race,
Brooded a moment as he hung
Over the crag-holds wearily,
And with the final echo, flung
His body to the Austral Sea.

Wilder than the maddest rout,
Madder than the wildest roar,
A storm of rage unknown before
Followed Tyrannus' passing out.
The dark unreason of his mind,
Read in promiscuous assault
Upon the land and ocean kind,
Had placed the agreement in default.
But through the day, the immediate sight
Of a teeming and aggressive sea
Enforced the covenantal right
Against a mutual enemy;
Kept in abeyance blood desires
As veteran as Jurassic fires.
Now under cover of the night
When many of their ranks had died
Of virus from the saurian's bite,
The leash of discipline was untied,
And soon the full abysmal sound
Broke out in internecine notes
From all the brutes on fighting ground
Feeling for each other's throats.
So piercing was the central cry
It carried to the southward high
Over the foothills to the crests
Of the snowy Guadeleras, waking
The æries of the eagles; shaking
The condors from their craggy nests.
Then by a fierce contagion carried
East and west to either tip
Of the Isthmian sea-board, it was harried
Into ten thousand shards; – the rip

Of lion's claws on buffalo hides;
Of ivory through the lions' sides;
The grunt of a bush hog or the squeal
Of a babyroussa with the pounce
Of an infuriated ounce;
Of leopards crushed beneath the kneel
Of battle-wearied elephants;
The growls of bears; the dissonance
Of fleeing, howling allouattes
Pursued by cheetahs; of wild cats
Nine-lived and strung in endless knots
Upon the backs of Cashmir ewes,
Or arguing with ocelots
The fallen bodies of kangaroos.
And now and then the storm would rise
To unimaginable cries,
As though a stubborn racial note,
Goaded to the bitter-full,
Had baulked within the cosmic throat.
And yet the scale, for all this woe,
Had still a higher note to go.

All through the day,–in throaty pant
Of steam and pulmonary moan,
Being full of slag, the stridulant
Jurania, like a surly crone,
Had growled about a deeper pain,
Caused by an old Silurian sprain.
By dusk, her fetid breath had grown
Into a thick revolving cone.
And as the minutes passed, a flash,–
An incandescent fork of blue,
And now of green would struggle through
The smothering pall of smoke and ash,
Until with undulating sheet
Of multi-coloured flame that beat
The blank face of the sky apart,–
Just as the last convulsive stroke
Unthrottled the volcano's heart,–
The storm flood of the lava broke.
It shot a fifteen thousand feet
Straight to the sky, then billowing higher,
And outward, made as if to meet
Its own maternal stellar fire

With tenuous play of finger streaks;
But failing in its vaunted leap,
Returned with frenzied haste to sweep
Across the Guadelera peaks;
Inundate the valleys; glut
The plains and canyons; rise and shut
The higher gorges, rifts and caves
Of the mountains; overflow and roll
Seaward with tumbling lava waves
Over the great Juranian bowl.
It blazed the forest pines and passed
The northern stretch of cliffs until,
Clearing the summit and the last
Excoriated ridge and hill,
It poured its fury on the dead;
Then the inexorable blast,
Capping the horrors of the night,
Pursued the living remnants, bled
To the final pulses with the fight,
And caught them as they tried to flee
To the drowning mercies of the sea.

Far to the East,—from all this dire
Titanic strife of claw and fire,
The only fighter to escape,—
The female anthropoidal ape!
By subtle powers that placed her head
Of land belligerents, she, alone,
Had often turned to watch with dread
The beat of catastrophic power,
In cloud and thunder, as the cone
Ticked off her last Aeonian hour.
She sniffed the warning just in time,
Before the extinction throe, to reach
The forest heights that flanked the beach.
She took the eastern headland climb,
And then turned southwards from the sea,
Shambling upward wearily,
Ever on the chasing fringe
Of the lava that, with hideous twist
Of myriad anacondas, hissed
And spat out fiery tongues to singe
Her hair. Gaining the summit where
Water breezes cooled the air,

She paused a moment to endure
The scene survived, her eyes aglow
Held first by the mesmeric lure
Of globes of vivid indigo
That danced and burst as they were thrown
From the deep labour of the cone,
And then by that which choked her breath
And dazed her brain, – the molten red
Of plain and ridge on which were spread
The incredulities of death,
Riding on tumultuously
In a gulf of fire to the sea.
Under the shelter of the height,
She gathered up her residue
Of will to blot out from her view
The awful fiction of the night,
And take upon herself the strain
Of the descent. By swinging, crawling,
Running in little spurts and falling,
Splay-footed, shoulders crooked with pain,
She reached a shallow river-bed
Winding through a moor which led
Her to a grove of sandalwood.
There, at the hollow of a tree,
She found her lair, and brokenly
She entered in, cuddling her brood
To withered paps; and in the hush
Of the laggard hours as the flush
Of dawn burnt out the coppery tones
That smeared the unfamiliar West,
The heralds of the day were moans,
And croons, and drummings of the breast.

The Highway

What aeons passed without a count or name,
Before the cosmic seneschal,
Succeeding with a plan
Of weaving stellar patterns from a flame,
Announced at his high carnival
An orbit – with Aldebaran!

And when the drifting years had sighted land,
And hills and plains declared their birth
Amid volcanic throes,
What was the lapse before the marshal's hand
Had found a garden on the earth,
And led forth June with her first rose?

And what the gulf between that and the hour,
Late in the simian-human day,
When Nature kept her tryst
With the unfoldment of the star and flower –
When in her sacrificial way
Judaea blossomed with her Christ!

But what made *our* feet miss that road that brought
The world to such a golden trove,
In our so brief a span?
How may we grasp again the hand that wrought
Such light, such fragrance, and such love,
O star! O rose! O Son of Man?

Come Away, Death

Willy-nilly, he comes or goes, with the clown's logic.
Comic in epitaph, tragic in epithalamium,
And unseduced by any mused rhyme.
However blow the winds over the pollen,
Whatever the course of the garden variables,
He remains the constant,
Ever flowering from the poppy seeds.

There was a time he came in formal dress,
Announced by Silence tapping at the panels
In deep apology.
A touch of chivalry in his approach,
He offered sacramental wine,
And with acanthus leaf
And petals of the hyacinth
He took the fever from the temples
And closed the eyelids,
Then led the way to his cool longitudes
In the dignity of the candles.

His mediaeval grace is gone –
Gone with the flame of the capitals
And the leisured turn of the thumb
Leafing the manuscripts,
Gone with the marbles
And the Venetian mosaics,
With the bend of the knee
Bèfore the rose-strewn feet of the Virgin.
The *paternosters* of his priests,
Committing clay to clay,
Have rattled in their throats
Under the gride of his traction tread.

One night we heard his footfall – one September night –
In the outskirts of a village near the sea.
There was a moment when the storm
Delayed its fist, when the surf fell
Like velvet on the rocks – a moment only;
The strangest lull we ever knew!
A sudden truce among the oaks
Released their fratricidal arms;
The poplars straightened to attention
As the winds stopped to listen
To the sound of a motor drone –
And then the drone was still.
We heard the tick-tock on the shelf,
And the leak of valves in our hearts.
As calm condensed and lidded
As at the core of a cyclone ended breathing
This was the monologue of Silence
Grave and unequivocal.

What followed was a bolt
Outside the range and target of the thunder,
And human speech curved back upon itself
Through Druid runways and the Piltdown scarps.
Beyond the stammers of the Java caves,
To find its origins in hieroglyphs.
On mouths and eyes and cheeks
Etched by a foreign stylus never used
On the outmoded page of the Apocalypse.

The Truant

"What have you there?" the great Panjandrum said
To the Master of the Revels who had led
A bucking truant with a stiff backbone
Close to the foot of the Almighty's throne.

"Right Reverend, most adored,
And forcibly acknowledged Lord
By the keen logic of your two-edged sword!
This creature has presumed to classify
Himself – a biped, rational, six feet high
And two feet wide; weighs fourteen stone;
Is guilty of a multitude of sins.
He has adjured his choric origins.
And like an undomesticated slattern,
Walks with tangential step unknown
Within the weave of the atomic pattern.
He has developed concepts, grins
Obscenely at your Royal bulletins,
Possesses what he calls a will
Which challenges your power to kill."

"What is his pedigree?"

'The base is guaranteed, your Majesty –
Calcium, carbon, phosphorus, vapour
And other fundamentals spun
From the umbilicus of the sun,
And yet he says he will not caper
Around your throne, nor toe the rules
For the ballet of the fiery molecules."
'His concepts and denials – scrap them, burn them –
To the chemists with them promptly."

                                    "Sire,
The stuff is not amenable to fire.
Nothing but their own kind can overturn them.
The chemists have sent back the same old story –
'With our extreme gelatinous apology,
We beg to inform your Imperial Majesty,
Unto whom be dominion and power and glory,
There still remains that strange precipitate
Which has the quality to resist
Our oldest and most trusted catalyst.
It is a substance we cannot cremate
By temperatures known to our Laboratory.'"

And the great Panjandrum's face grew dark—
'I'll put those chemists to their annual purge,
And I myself shall be the thaumaturge
To find the nature of this fellow's spark.
Come, bring him nearer by yon halter rope:
I'll analyse him with the cosmoscope."
Pulled forward with his neck awry,
The little fellow six feet short,
Aware he was about to die,
Committed grave contempt of court
By answering with a flinchless stare
The Awful Presence seated there.

The ALL HIGH swore until his face was black.
He called him a coprophagite,
A genus *homo*, egomaniac,
Third cousin to the family of worms.
A sporozoan from the ooze of night,
Spawn of a spavined troglodyte:
He swore by all the catalogue of terms
Known since the slang of carboniferous Time.
He said that he could trace him back
To pollywogs and earwigs in the slime.
And in his shrillest tenor he began
Reciting his indictment of the man,
Until he closed upon this capital crime—
'You are accused of singing out of key,
(A foul unmitigated dissonance)
Of shuffling in the measures of the dance,
Then walking out with that defiant, free
Toss of your head, banging the doors,
Leaving a stench upon the jacinth floors.
You have fallen like a curse
On the mechanics of my Universe.

"Herewith I measure out your penalty—
Hearken while you hear, look while you see:
I send you now upon your homeward route
Where you shall find
Humiliation for your pride of mind.
I shall make deaf the ear, and dim the eye,
Put palsy in your touch, make mute
Your speech, intoxicate your cells and dry
Your blood and marrow, shoot

Arthritic needles through your cartilage,
And having parched you with old age,
I'll pass you wormwise through the mire;
And when your rebel will
Is mouldered, all desire
Shrivelled, all your concepts broken,
Backward in dust I'll blow you till
You join my spiral festival of fire.
Go, Master of the Revels – I have spoken."
And the little genus *homo*, six feet high,
Standing erect, countered with this reply –
"You dumb insouciant invertebrate,
You rule a lower than a feudal state –
A realm of flunkey decimals that run,
Return; return and run; again return,
Each group around its little sun,
And every sun a satellite.
There they go by day and night,
Nothing to do but run and burn,
Taking turn and turn about,
Light-year in and light-year out,
Dancing, dancing in quadrillons,
Never leaving their pavilions.

"Your astronomical conceit
Of bulk and power is anserine.
Your ignorance so thick,
You did not know your own arithmetic.
We flung the graphs about your flying feet;
We measured your diameter –
Merely a line
Of zeros prefaced by an integer.
Before we came
You had no name.
You did not know direction or your pace;
We taught you all you ever knew
Of motion, time and space.
We healed you of your vertigo
And put you in our kindergarten show,
Perambulated you through prisms, drew
Your mileage through the Milky Way,
Lassoed your comets when they ran astray,
Yoked Leo, Taurus, and your team of Bears
To pull our kiddy cars of inverse squares.

"Boast not about your harmony,
  Your perfect curves, your rings
Of *pure and endless light*–'Twas we
Who pinned upon your Seraphim their wings,
And when your brassy heavens rang
With joy that morning while the planets sang
Their choruses of archangelic lore,
'Twas we who ordered the notes upon their score
Out of our winds and strings.
  Yes! all your shapely forms
Are ours–parabolas of silver light,
Those blueprints of your spiral stairs
From nadir depth to zenith height,
Coronas, rainbows after storms,
Auroras on your eastern tapestries
And constellations over western seas.

"And when, one day, grown conscious of your age,
  While pondering an eolith,
We turned a human page
And blotted out a cosmic myth
With all its baby symbols to explain
The sunlight in Apollo's eyes,
Our rising pulses and the birth of pain,
Fear, and that fern-and-fungus breath
Stalking our nostrils to our caves of death–
That day we learned how to anatomize
Your body, calibrate your size
And set a mirror up before your face
To show you what you really were–a rain
Of dull Lucretian atoms crowding space,
A series of concentric waves which any fool
Might make by dropping stones within a pool,
Or an exploding bomb forever in flight
Bursting like hell through Chaos and Old Night.

"You oldest of the hierarchs
  Composed of electronic sparks,
We grant you speed,
We grant you power, and fire
That ends in ash, but we concede
To you no pain nor joy nor love nor hate.
No final tableau of desire,
No causes won or lost, no free

Adventure at the outposts – only
The degradation of your energy
When at some late
Slow number of your dance your sergeant-major Fate
Will catch you blind and groping and will send
You reeling on that long and lonely
Lockstep of your wave-lengths towards your end.

"We who have met
With stubborn calm the dawn's hot fusillades;
Who have seen the forehead sweat
Under the tug of pulleys on the joints,
Under the liquidating tally
Of the cat-and-truncheon bastinades;
Who have taught our souls to rally
To mountain horns and the sea's rockets
When the needle ran demented through the points;
We who have learned to clench
Our fists and raise our lightless sockets
To morning skies after the midnight raids,
Yet cocked our ears to bugles on the barricades,
And in cathedral rubble found a way to quench
A dying thirst within a Galilean valley –
No! by the Rood, we will not join your ballet."

Towards the Last Spike

It was the same world then as now – the same,
Except for little differences of speed
And power, and means to treat myopia
To show an axe-blade infinitely sharp
Splitting things infinitely small, or else
Provide the telescopic sight to roam
Through curved dominions never found in fables.
The same, but for new particles of speech –
Those algebraic substitutes for nouns
That sky cartographers would hang like signboards
Along the trespass of our thoughts to stop
The stutters of our tongues with their equations.

As now, so then, blood kept its ancient colour,
And smoothly, roughly, paced its banks; in calm
Preserving them, in riot rupturing them.
Wounds needed bandages and stomachs food:
The hands outstretched had joined the lips in prayer –
"Give us our daily bread, give us our pay."
The past flushed in the present and tomorrow
Would dawn upon today: only the rate
To sensitize or numb a nerve would change;
Only the quickening of a measuring skill
To gauge the onset of a birth or death
With the precision of micrometers.
Men spoke of acres then and miles and masses,
Velocity and steam, cables that moored
Not ships but continents, world granaries,
The east-west cousinship, a nation's rise,
Hail of identity, a world expanding,
If not the universe: the feel of it
Was in the air – *"Union required the Line."*
The theme was current at the banquet tables,
And argument profane and scarlet rent
God-fearing families into partisans.
Pulpit, platform and floor were sounding-boards·
Cushions beneath the pounding fists assumed
The hues of western sunsets; nostrils sniffed
The prairie tang; the tongue rolled over texts:
Even St. Paul was being invoked to wring
The neck of Thomas in this war of faith
With unbelief. Was ever an adventure
Without its cost? Analogies were found
On every page of history or science.
A nation, like the world, could not stand still.
What was the use of records but to break them?
The tougher armour followed the new shell;
The newer shell the armour; lighthouse rockets
Sprinkled their stars over the wake of wrecks.
Were not the engineers at work to close
The lag between the pressures and the valves?
The same world then as now thirsting for power
To crack those records open, extra pounds
Upon the inches, extra miles per hour.
The mildewed static schedules which before
Had like asbestos been immune to wood

Now curled and blackened in the furnace coal.
This power lay in the custody of men
From down-and-outers needing roofs, whose hands
Were moulded by their fists, whose skins could feel
At home incorporate with dolomite,
To men who with the marshal instincts in them,
Deriving their authority from wallets,
Directed their battalions from the trestles.

THE GATHERING

*("Oats—a grain which in England is generally
given to horses, but in Scotland supports the
people."—Dr. Samuel Johnson. "True, but where
will you find such horses, where such men?"—
Lord Elibank's reply as recorded by Sir Walter
Scott.)*

Oatmeal was in their blood and in their names.
Thrift was the title of their catechism.
It governed all things but their mess of porridge
Which, when it struck the hydrochloric acid
With treacle and skim-milk, became a mash.
Entering the duodenum, it broke up
Into amino acids: then the liver
Took on its natural job as carpenter:
Foreheads grew into cliffs, jaws into juts.
The meal, so changed, engaged the follicles:
Eyebrows came out as gorse, the beards as thistles,
And the chest-hair the fell of Grampian rams.
It stretched and vulcanized the human span:
Nonagenarians worked and thrived upon it.
Out of such chemistry run through by genes,
The food released its fearsome racial products:—
The power to strike a bargain like a foe,
To win an argument upon a burr,
Invest the language with a Bannockburn,
Culloden or the warnings of Lochiel,
Weave loyalties and rivalries in tartans,
Present for the amazement of the world
Kilts and the civilized barbaric Fling,
And pipes which, when they acted on the mash,
Fermented lullabies to *Scots wha hae*.

Their names were like a battle-muster – Angus
(He of the Shops) and Fleming (of the Transit),
Hector (of the *Kicking Horse*), Dawson,
"Cromarty" Ross, and Beatty (Ulster Scot),
Bruce, Allan, Galt and Douglas, and the "twa" –
Stephen (Craigellachie)* and Smith (Strathcona) –
Who would one day climb from their Gaelic hide-outs,
Take off their plaids and wrap them round the mountains.
And then the everlasting tread of the Macs,
Vanguard, centre and rear, their roving eyes
On summits, rivers, contracts, beaver, ledgers;
Their ears cocked to the skirl of Sir John A.,
The general of the patronymic march.

*(Sir John revolving round the Terms of Union with
British Columbia. Time, late at night.)*

Insomnia had ripped the bed-sheets from him
Night after night. How long was this to last?
Confederation had not played this kind
Of trickery on him. That was rough indeed,
So gravelled, that a man might call for rest
And take it for a life accomplishment.
It was his laurel though some of the leaves
'Had dried. But this would be a longer tug
Of war which needed for his team thick wrists
And calloused fingers, heavy heels to dig
Into the earth and hold – men with bull's beef
Upon their ribs. Had he himself the wind,
The anchor-waist to peg at the rope's end?
'Twas bad enough to have these questions hit
The waking mind: 'twas much worse when he dozed;
For goblins had a way of pinching him,
Slapping a nightmare on to dwindling snoozes.
They put him and his team into a tug
More real than life. He heard a judge call out –
"Teams settle on the rope and take the strain!"
And with the coaches' *heave*, the running welts
Reddened his palms, and then the gruelling *backlock*

*"*Stand Fast, Craigellachie*," the war-cry of the Clan
Grant, named after a rock in the Spey Valley, and
used as a cable message from Stephen in London to
the Directors in Montreal.

Inscribed its indentations on his shoulders.
This kind of burn he knew he had to stand;
It was the game's routine; the other fire
Was that he feared the most for it could bake him—
That white dividing rag tied to the rope
Above the centre pole had with each heave
Wavered with chances equal. With the backlock,
Despite the legs of Tupper and Cartier,
The western anchor dragged; the other side
Remorselessly was gaining, holding, gaining.
No sleep could stand this strain and, with the nightmare
Delivered of its colt, Macdonald woke.

Tired with the midnight toss, lock-jawed with yawns,
He left the bed and, shuffling to the window,
He opened it. The air would cool him off
And soothe his shoulder burns. He felt his ribs:
Strange, nothing broken—how those crazy drowses
Had made the fictions tangle with the facts!
He must unscramble them with steady hands.
Those Ranges pirouetting in his dreams
Had their own knack of standing still in light,
Revealing peaks whose known triangulation
Had to be read in prose severity.
Seizing a telescope, he swept the skies,
The north-south drift, a self-illuminated chart.
Under Polaris was the Arctic Sea
And the sub-Arctic gates well stocked with names:
Hudson, Davis, Baffin, Frobisher;
And in his own day Franklin, Ross and Parry
Of the Canadian Archipelago;
Kellett, McClure, McClintock, of *The Search*.
Those straits and bays had long been kicked by keels,
And flags had fluttered on the Capes that fired
His youth, making familiar the unknown.
What though the odds were nine to one against,
And the Dead March was undertoning trumpets,
There was enough of strychnine in the names
To make him flip a penny for the risk,
Though he had palmed the coin reflectively
Before he threw and watched it come down *heads*.
That stellar path looked too much like a road map
Upon his wall—the roads all led to market—
The north-south route. He lit a candle, held

It to a second map full of blank spaces
And arrows pointing west. Disturbed, he turned
The lens up to the zenith, followed the course
Tracked by a cloud of stars that would not keep
Their posts – Capella, Perseus, were reeling;
Low in the north-west, Cassiopeia
Was qualmish, leaning on her starboard arm-rest,
And Aries was chasing, butting Cygnus,
Just diving. Doubts and hopes struck at each other.
Why did those constellations look so much
Like blizzards? And what lay beyond the blizzards?

'Twas chilly at the window. He returned
To bed and savoured soporific terms:
Superior, the *Red River, Selkirk, Prairie,*
Port Moody and *Pacific*. Chewing them,
He spat out *Rocky* grit before he swallowed.
Selkirk! This had the sweetest taste. Ten years
Before, the Highland crofters had subscribed
Their names in a memorial for the Rails.
Sir John reviewed the story of the struggle,
That four months' journey from their native land –
The Atlantic through the Straits to Hudson Bay,
Then the Hayes River to Lake Winnipeg
Up to the Forks of the Assiniboine.
He could make use of that – just what he needed,
A Western verision of the Arctic daring,
Romance and realism, double dose.
How long ago? Why, this is '71.
Those fellows came the time Napoleon
Was on the steppes. For sixty years they fought
The seasons, 'hoppers, drought, hail, wind and snow;
Survived the massacre at Seven Oaks,
The "Pemmican War" and the Red River floods.
They wanted now the Road – those pioneers
Who lived by spades instead of beaver traps.
Most excellent word that, pioneers! Sir John
Snuggled himself into his sheets, rolling
The word around his tongue, a theme for song,
Or for a peroration to a speech.

THE HANGOVER AT DAWN

He knew the points that had their own appeal.
These did not bother him: the patriot touch,
The Flag, the magnetism of explorers,
The national unity. These could burn up
The phlegm in most of the provincial throats.
But there was one tale central to his plan
(The focus of his headache at this moment),
Which would demand the limit of his art—
The ballad of his courtship in the West:
Better reveal it soon without reserve.

THE LADY OF BRITISH COLUMBIA

Port Moody and Pacific! He had pledged
His word the Line should run from sea to sea.
"From sea to sea", a hallowed phrase. Music
Was in that text if the right key were struck,
And he must strike it first, for, as he fingered
The clauses of the pledge, rough notes were rasping—
"No Road, No Union", and the converse true.
East-west against the north-south run of trade,
For California like a sailor-lover
Was wooing over-time. He knew the ports.
His speech was as presuasive as his arms,
As sinuous as Spanish arias—
Tamales, Cazadero, Mendecino,
Curling their baritones around the Lady.
Then Santa Rosa, Santa Monica,
Held absolution in their syllables.
But when he saw her stock of British temper
Starch at ironic sainthood in the whispers—
*"Rio de nuestra señora de buena guia,"**
He had the tact to gutturalize the liquids,
Steeping the tunes to drinking songs, then take
Her on a holiday where she could watch
A roving sea-born Californian pound
A downy chest and swear by San Diego.

"River of Our Lady of Safe Conduct."

Sir John, wise to the tricks, was studying hard
A fresh proposal for a marriage contract.
He knew a game was in the ceremony.
That southern fellow had a healthy bronze
Complexion, had a vast estate, was slick
Of manner. In this ardour he could tether
Sea-roses to the blossoms of his orchards,
And for his confidence he had the prime
Advantage of his rival – *he was there.*

THE LONG-DISTANCE PROPOSAL

A game it was, and the Pacific lass
Had poker wisdom on her face. Her name
Was rich in values – *British*; this alone
Could raise Macdonald's temperature: so could
Columbia with a different kind of fever,
And in between the two, *Victoria*.
So the *Pacific* with its wash of letters
Could push the Fahrenheit another notch.
She watched for bluff on those Disraeli features,
Impassive but for arrowy chipmunk eyes,
Engaged in fathoming a contract time.
With such a dowry she could well afford
To take the risk of tightening the terms –
"Begin the Road in two years, end in ten" –
Sir John, a moment letting down his guard,
Frowned at the Rocky skyline, but agreed.

*(The Terms ratified by Parliament, British Co-
lumbia enters Confederation July, 1871, Sandford
Fleming being appointed engineer-in-chief of the
proposed Railway, Walter Moberly to co-operate
with him in the location of routes. "Of course,
I don't know how many millions you have, but
it is going to cost you money to get through
those canyons." – Moberly to Macdonald.)*

THE PACIFIC SCANDAL

*(Huntingdon's charges of political corruption
based on correspondence and telegrams rifled
from the offices of the solicitor of Sir Hugh
Allan, Head of the Canada Pacific Company;
Sir John's defence; and the appearance of the
Honourable Edward Blake who rises to reply to
Sir John at 2 a.m.)*

BLAKE IN MOOD

Of all the subjects for debate here was
His element. His soul as clean as surf,
No one could equal him in probing cupboards
Or sweeping floors and dusting shelves, finding
A skeleton inside an overcoat;
Or shaking golden eagles from a pocket
To show the copper plugs within the coins.
Rumours he heard had gangrened into facts –
Gifts nuzzling at two-hundred-thousand dollars,
Elections on, and with a contract pending.
The odour of the bills had blown his gorge.
His appetite, edged by a moral hone,
Could surfeit only on the Verities.

November 3, 1873

A Fury rode him to the House. He took
His seat, and with a stoic gloom he heard
The Chieftain's great defence and noted well
The punctuation of the cheers. He needed all
The balance of his mind to counterpoise
The movements of Macdonald as he flung
Himself upon the House, upon the Country,
Upon posterity, upon his conscience.
That plunging played the devil with Blake's tiller,
Threatened the set of his sail. To save the course,
To save himself, in that five hours of gale,
He had to jettison his meditation,
His brooding on the follies of mankind,
Clean out the wadding from his tortured ears:

That roaring mob before him could be quelled
Only by action; so when the last round
Of the applause following the peroration
Was over, slowly, weightily, Blake rose.

A statesman-chancellor now held the Floor.
He told the sniffing Commons that a sense
Keener than smell or taste must be invoked
To get the odour. Leading them from facts
Like telegrams and stolen private letters,
He soared into the realm of principles
To find his scourge; and then the men involved,
Robed like the Knights of Malta, Blake undressed,
Their cloaks inverted to reveal the shoddy,
The tattered lining and bare-threaded seams.
He ripped the last stitch from them – by the time
Recess was called, he had them in the dock
As brigands in the Ministry of Smells,
Naked before the majesty of Heaven.

For Blake recesses were but sandwiches
Provided merely for cerebral luncheons –
No time to spread the legs under the table,
To chat and chaff a while, to let the mind
Roam, like a goblet up before the light
To bask in natural colour, or by whim
Of its own choice to sway luxuriously
In tantalizing arcs before the nostrils.
A meal was meant by Nature for nutrition –
A sorry farinaceous business scaled
Exactly to caloric grains and grams
Designed for intellectual combustion,
For energy directed into words
Towards proof. Abuse was overweight. He saw
No need for it; no need for caricature,
And if a villainous word had to be used,
'Twas for a villain – keen upon the target.
Irrelevance was like a moral lesion
No less within a speech than in a statute.
What mattered it who opened up the files,
Sold for a bid the damning correspondence –
That Montreal-Chicago understanding?
A dirty dodge, so let it be conceded.

But *here* the method was irrelevant.
Whether by legal process or by theft,
The evidence was there unalterable.
So with the House assembled, he resumed
Imperial indictment of the bandits.
The logic left no loopholes in the facts.
Figures that ran into the hundred-thousands
Were counted up in pennies, each one shown
To bear the superscription of debasement.

Again recess, again the sandwiches,
Again the invocation of the gods:
Each word, each phrase, each clause went to position,
Each sentence regimented like a lockstep.
The only thing that would not pace was time;
The hours dragged by until the thrushes woke –
Two days, two nights – someone opened a window,
And members of the House who still were conscious
Uncreaked their necks to note that even Sir John
Himself had put his fingers to his nose.

*(The appeal to the country: Macdonald defeated:
Mackenzie assumes power, 1874.)*

A change of air, a drop in temperature!
The House had rarely known sobriety
Like this. No longer clanged the *"Westward Ho!"*
And quiet were the horns upon the hills.
Hard times ahead. The years were rendering up
Their fat. Measured and rationed was the language
Directed to the stringency of pockets.
The eye must be convinced before the *vision.*
"But one step at a time," exclaimed the feet.
It was the story of the hen or egg;
Which came before the other? *"'Twas the hen,"*
Cried one; *"undoubtedly the hen must lay
The egg, hatch it and mother it." "Not so,"*
Another shouted, *"'Twas the egg or whence
The hen?"* For every one who cleared his throat
And called across the House with Scriptural passion –
"The Line is meant to bring the loaves and fishes,"
A voting three had countered with the question –
"Where are the multitudes that thirst and hunger?"
Passion became displaced by argument.

Till now the axles justified their grease,
Taught coal a lesson in economy.
All doubts here could be blanketed with facts,
With phrases smooth as actuarial velvet.

For forty years in towns and cities men
Had watched the Lines baptized with charters, seen
Them grow, marry and bring forth children.
Parades and powder had their uses then
For gala days; and bands announced arrivals,
Betrothals, wedding and again arrivals.
Champagne brimmed in the font as they were named
With titles drawn from the explorers' routes,
From Saints and Governors, from space and seas
And compass-points – Saints Andrew, Lawrence, Thomas,
Louis and John; Champlain, Simcoe; Grand Trunk,
Intercolonial, the Canadian Southern,
Dominion-Atlantic, the Great Western – names
That caught a continental note and tried
To answer it. Half-gambles though they were,
Directors built those Roads and heard them run
To the sweet silver jingle in their minds.

The airs had long been mastered like old songs
The feet could tap to in the galleries.
But would they tap to a new rhapsody,
A harder one to learn and left unfinished?
What ear could be assured of absolute pitch
To catch this kind of music in the West?
The far West? Men had used this flattering name
For East or but encroachment on the West.
And was not Lake Superior still the East,
A natural highway which ice-ages left,
An unappropriated legacy?
There was no discord in the piston-throbs
Along this Road. This was old music too.
That northern spine of rock, those western mountains,
Were barriers built of God and cursed of Blake.
Mild in his oaths, Mackenzie would avoid them.
He would let contracts for the south and west,
Push out from settlement to settlement.
This was economy, just plain horse-sense.
The Western Lines were there – American.

The Eagle and the Lion were good friends:
At least the two could meet on sovereign terms
Without a sign of fur and feathers flying.
As yet, but who could tell? So far, so good.
Spikes had been driven at the boundary line,
From Emerson across the Red to Selkirk,
And then to Thunder Bay – to Lake Superior;
Across the prairies in God's own good time,
His plodding, patient, planetary time.

Five years' delay: surveys without construction;
Short lines suspended, discord in the Party.
The West defrauded of its glittering peaks,
The public blood was stirring and protesting
At this continuous dusk upon the mountains.
The old conductor off the podium,
The orchestra disbanded at the time
The daring symphony was on the score,
The audience cupped their ears to catch a strain:
They heard a plaintive thinning oboe-A
That kept on thinning while slow feeble steps
Approached the stand. Was this the substitute
For what the auditorium once knew –
The maestro who with tread of stallion hoofs
Came forward shaking platforms and the rafters,
And followed up the concert pitch with sound
Of drums and trumpets and the organ blasts
That had the power to toll out apathy
And make snow peaks ring like Cathedral steeples?
Besides, accompanying those bars of music,
There was an image men had not forgotten,
The shaggy chieftain standing at his desk,
That last-ditch fight when he was overthrown,
That desperate five hours. At least they knew
His personal pockets were not lined with pelf,
Whatever loot the others grabbed. The words
British, the West instead of South, the Nation,
The all-Canadian route – these terms were singing
Fresher than ever while the grating tones
Under the stress of argument had faded
Within the shroud of their monotony.

*(Sir John returns to power in 1878 with a
National Policy of Protective Tariff and the
Transcontinental.)*

Two years of tuning up: it needed that
To counterpoint Blake's eloquence or lift
Mackenzie's non-adventurous common sense
To the ignition of an enterprise.
The pace had to be slow at first, a tempo
Cautious, simple to follow. Sections strewn
Like amputated limbs along the route
Were sutured. This appeal to sanity.
No argument could work itself to sweat
Against a prudent case, for the terrain
Looked easy from the Lake to the Red River.
To stop with those suspensions was a waste
Of cash and time. But the huge task announced
Ten years before had now to start afresh –
The moulding of men's minds was harder far
Than moulding of the steel and prior to it.
It was the battle of ideas and words
And kindred images called by the same name,
Like brothers who with temperamental blood
Went to it with their fists. Canyons and cliffs
Were precipices down which men were hurled,
Or something to be bridged and sheared and scaled.
Likewise the Pass had its ambiguous meaning.
The leaders of the factions in the House
And through the country spelled the word the same:
The way they got their tongue around the word
Was different, for some could make it hiss
With sound of blizzards screaming over ramparts:
The Pass – the Yellowhead, the Kicking Horse –
Or jam it with *coureur-de-bois* romance,
Or join it to the empyrean. Eagles,
In flight banking their wings above a fish-stream,
Had guided the explorers to a route
And given the Pass the title of their wings.
The stories lured men's minds up to the mountains
And down along the sandbars of the rivers.
Rivalling the "*brown and barren*" on the maps,
Officially "*not fit for human life*",
Were vivid yellows flashing in the news –
"*Gold in the Cariboo,*" "*Gold in the Fraser.*"

The swish of gravel in the placer-cradles
Would soon be followed by the spluttering fuses,
By thunder echoing thunder; for one month
After Blake's Ottawa roar would Onderdonk
Roar back from Yale by ripping canyon walls
To crash the tons by millions in the gorges.

The farther off, as by a paradox
Of magnets, was the golden lure the stronger:
Two thousand miles away, imagined peaks
Had the vacation pull of mountaineering,
But with the closer vision would the legs
Follow the mind? 'Twas Blake who raised the question
And answered it. Though with his natural eyes
Up to this time he had not sighted mountains,
He was an expert with the telescope.

THE ATTACK

Sir John was worried. The first hour of Blake
Was dangerous, granted the theme. Eight years
Before, he had the theme combined with language.
Impeachment–word with an historic ring,
Reserved for the High Courts of Parliament,
Uttered only when men were breathing hard
And when the vertebrae were musket-stiff:
High ground was that for his artillery,
And *there*, despite the hours the salvos lasted.
But *here* this was a theme less vulnerable
To fire, Macdonald thought, to Blake's gunfire,
And yet he wondered what the orator
Might spring in that first hour, what strategy
Was on the Bench. He did not mind the close
Mosaic of the words – too intricate,
Too massive in design. Men might admire
The speech and talk about it, then forget it.
But few possessed the patience or the mind
To tread the mazes of the labyrinth.
Once in a while, however, would Blake's logic
Stumble upon stray figures that would leap
Over the walls of other folds and catch
The herdsmen in their growing somnolence.
The waking sound was not – "*It can't be done*",

That was a dogma, anyone might say it.
It was the following burning corollary:
"To build a Road over that sea of mountains."
This carried more than argument. It was
A flash of fire which might with proper kindling
Consume its way into the public mind.
The House clicked to the ready and Sir John,
Burying his finger-nails into his palms,
Muttered—*"God send us no more metaphors
Like that—except from Tory factories."*

Had Blake the lift of Chatham as he had
Burke's wind and almost that sierra span
Of mind, he might have carried the whole House
With him and posted it upon that sea
Of mountains with sub-zero on their scalps,
Their glacial ribs waiting for warmth of season
To spring an avalanche. Such similies
Might easily glue the members to their seats
With frost in preparation for their ride.
Sir John's *"from sea to sea"* was Biblical;
It had the stamp of reverent approval;
But Blake's was pagan, frightening, congealing.
The chieftain's lips continued as in prayer,
A fiercely secular and torrid prayer—
*"May Heaven intervene to stop the flow
Of such unnatural images and send
The rhetorician back to decimals,
Back to his tessellated subtleties."*
The prayer was answered for High Heaven did it.
The second hour entered and passed by,
A third, a fourth. Sir John looked round the House,
Noticed the growing shuffle of the feet,
The agony of legs, the yawn's contagion.
Was that a snore? Who was it that went out?
He glanced at the Press Gallery. The pens
Were scratching through the languor of the ink
To match the words with shorthand and were failing.
He hoped the speech would last another hour,
And still another. Well within the law,
This homicidal master of the opiates
Loosened the hinges of the Opposition:
The minds went first; the bodies sagged; the necks
Curved on the benches and the legs sprawled out.

And when the Fundy Tide had ebbed, Sir John,
Smiling, watched the debris upon the banks,
For what were yesterday grey human brains
Had with decomposition taken on
The texture and complexion of red clay.

(In 1880 Tupper lets contract to Onderdonk for
survey and construction through the Pacific Sec-
tion of the mountains. Sir John, Tupper, Pope,
and McIntyre go to London to interest capital
but return without a penny.)

Failing to make a dent in London dams,
Sir John set out to plumb a reservoir
Closer in reach. He knew its area,
Its ownership, the thickness of its banks,
Its conduits – if he could get his hands
Upon the local stopcocks, could he turn them?
The reservoir was deep. Two centuries
Ago it started filling when a king
Had in a furry moment scratched a quill
Across the bottom of His Royal Charter –
"Granting the Governor and His Company
Of Gentlemen Adventurers the right
Exclusive to one-third a continent."
Was it so easy then? A scratch, a seal,
A pinch of snuff tickling the sacred nostrils,
A puff of powder and the ink was dry.
Sir John twisted his lips: he thought of London.
Empire and wealth were in that signature
For royal, princely, ducal absentees,
For courtiers to whom the parallels
Were nothing but chalk scratches on a slate.
For them wild animals were held in game
Preserves, foxes as quarry in a chase,
And hills were hedges, river banks were fences,
And cataracts but fountains in a garden
Tumbling their bubbles into marble basins.
Where was this place called Hudson Bay? Some place
In the Antipodes? Explorers, traders,
Would bring their revenues over that signet.
Two centuries – the new empire advanced,
Was broken, reunited, torn again.

The *fleur-de-lis* went to half-mast, the *Jack*
To the mast-head, but fresher rivalries
Broke out – Nor'-Westers at the Hudson's throat
Over the pelts, over the pemmican;
No matter what – the dividends flowed in
As rum flowed out like the Saskatchewan.

The twist left Sir John's lips and he was smiling.
Though English in ambition and design,
This reservoir, he saw there in control
Upon the floodgates not a Londoner
In riding breeches but, red-flannel-shirted,
Trousered in homespun, streaked and blobbed with seal-oil,
A Scot with smoke of peat fire on his breath –
Smith? Yes: but christened Donald Alexander
And loined through issue from the Grants and Stuarts.

To smite the rock and bring forth living water,
Take lead or tin and transmute both to silver,
Copper to gold, betray a piece of glass
To diamonds, fabulize a continent,
Were wonders once believed, scrapped and revived;
For Moses, Marco Polo, Paracelsus,
Fell in the same retort and came out *Smith*.
A miracle on legs, the lad had left
Forres and Aberdeen, gone to Lachine –
"Tell Mr. Smith to count and sort the rat-skins."
Thence Tadoussac and Posts off Anticosti;
From there to Rigolet in Labrador,
A thousand miles by foot, snowshoe and dog-sled.
He fought the climate like a weathered yak,
And conquered it, ripping the stalactites
From his red beard, thawing his feet, and wringing
Salt water from his mitts; but most of all
He learned the art of making change. Blankets,
Ribbons and beads, tobacco, guns and knives,
Were swapped for muskrat, marten, fox and beaver.
And when the fur trade thinned, he trapped the salmon,
Canned it; hunted the seal, traded its oil
And fertilized the gardens with the carcass.
Even the melons grew in Labrador.
What could resist this touch? Water from rock!
Why not? No more a myth than pelts should be
Thus fabricated into bricks of gold.

If rat-skins, why not tweeds? If looms could take
Raw wool and twill it into selling shape,
They could under the draper's weaving mind
Be patterning gold braid:

                      So thought George Stephen.

His legs less sturdy than his cousin Donald's,
His eyes were just as furiously alert.
His line of vision ran from the north-west
To the Dutch-held St. Paul-Pacific Railway.
Allied with Smith, Kitson and Kennedy,
Angus, Jim Hill and Duncan McIntyre,
Could he buy up this semi-bankrupt Road
And turn the northern traffic into it?
Chief bricklayer of all the Scotian clans,
And foremost as a banking metallurgist,
He took the parchments at their lowest level
And mineralized them, roasted them to shape,
Then mortared them into the pyramid,
Till with the trowel-stretching exercise
He grew so Atlas-strong that he could carry
A mountain like a namesake on his shoulders.

(*The Charter granted to The Canadian Pacific
Railway, February 17, 1881, with George Stephen
as first President . . . One William Cornelius
Van Horne arrives in Winnipeg, December 31,
1881, and there late at night, forty below zero,
gives vent to a soliloquy.*)

Stephen had laid his raw hands on Van Horne,
Pulled him across the border, sent him up
To get the feel of northern temperatures.
He knew through Hill the story of his life
And found him made to order. Nothing less
Than geologic space his field of work,
He had in Illinois explored the creeks
And valleys, brooded on the rocks and quarries.
Using slate fragments, he became a draughtsman,
Bringing to life a landscape or a cloud,
Turning a tree into a beard, a cliff
Into a jaw, a creek into a mouth
With banks for lips. He loved to work on shadows.
Just now the man was forcing the boy's stature,

The while the youth tickled the man within.
Companioned by the shade of Agassiz,
He would come home, his pockets stuffed with fossils—
Crinoids and fish-teeth – and his tongue jabbering
Of the earth's crust before the birth of life,
Prophetic of the days when he would dig
Into Laurentian rock. The Morse-key tick
And tape were things mesmeric – space and time
Had found a junction. Electricity
And rock, one novel to the coiling hand,
The other frozen in the lap of age,
Were playthings for the boy, work for the man.
As man he was the State's first operator;
As boy he played a trick upon his boss
Who, cramped with current, fired him on the instant;
As man at school, escaping Latin grammar,
He tore the fly-leaf from the text to draw
The contour of a hill; as boy he sketched
The principal, gave him flapdoodle ears,
Bristled his hair, turned eyebrows into quills,
His whiskers into flying buttresses,
His eye-tusks into rusted railroad spikes,
And made a truss between his nose and chin.
Expelled again, he went back to the keys,
To bush and rock and found companionship
With quarry-men, stokers and station-masters,
Switchmen and locomotive engineers.

Now he was transferred to Winnipeg.
Of all the places in an unknown land
Chosen by Stephen for Van Horne, this was
The pivot on which he could turn his mind.
Here he could clap the future on the shoulder
And order Fate about as his lieutenant,
For he would take no nonsense from a thing
Called Destiny – the stars had to be with him.
He spent the first night in soliloquy,
Like Sir John A. but with a difference.
Sir John wanted to sleep but couldn't do it:
Van Horne could sleep but never wanted to.
It was a waste of time, his bed a place
Only to think or dream with eyes awake.
Opening a jack-knife, he went to the window,
Scraped off the frost. Great treks ran through his mind,

East-west. Two centuries and a half gone by,
One trek had started from the Zuyder Zee
To the new Amsterdam. 'Twas smooth by now,
Too smooth. His line of grandsires and their cousins
Had built a city from Manhattan dirt.
Another trek to Illinois; it too
Was smooth, but this new one it was his job
To lead, then build a highway which men claimed
Could not be built. Statesmen and engineers
Had blown their faces blue with their denials:
The men who thought so were asylum cases
Whose monomanias harmless up to now
Had not swept into cells. His bearded chin
Pressed to the pane, his eyes roved through the west.
He saw the illusion at its worst – the frost,
The steel precision of the studded heavens,
Relentless mirror of a covered earth.
His breath froze on the scrape: he cut again
And glanced at the direction west-by-south.
That westward trek was the American,
Union-Pacific – easy so he thought,
Their forty million stacked against his four.
Lonely and desolate this. He stocked his mind
With items of his task: the simplest first,
Though hard enough, the Prairies, then the Shore
North of the Lake – a quantity half-guessed.
Mackenzie like a balky horse had shied
And stopped at this. Van Horne knew well the reason,
But it was vital for the all-land route.
He peered through at the South. Down there Jim Hill
Was whipping up his horses on a road
Already paved. The stations offered rest
With food and warmth, and their well-rounded names
Were tossed like apples to the public taste.

He made a mental note of his three items.
He underlined the Prairies, double-lined
The Shore and triple-lined *Beyond the Prairies*,
Began counting the Ranges – first the Rockies;
The Kicking Horse ran through them, this he knew;
The Selkirks? Not so sure. Some years before
Had Moberly and Perry tagged a route
Across the lariat loop of the Columbia.
Now Rogers was traversing it on foot,

Reading an aneroid and compass, chewing
Sea-biscuit and tobacco. Would the steel
Follow this trail? Van Horne looked farther west.
There was the Gold Range, there the Coastal Mountains.
He stopped, putting a period to the note,
As rivers troubled nocturnes in his ears.
His plans must not seep into introspection –
Call it a night, for morning was at hand,
And every hour of daylight was for work.

(Van Horne goes to Montreal to meet the
Directors.)

He had agenda staggering enough
To bring the sweat even from Stephen's face.
As daring as his plans, so daring were
His promises. To build five hundred miles
Upon the prairies in one season: this
Was but a cushion for the jars ahead.
The Shore – he had to argue, stamp and fight
For this. The watercourses had been favoured,
The nation schooled to that economy.
He saw that Stephen, after wiping beads
From face and forehead, had put both his hands
Deep in his pockets – just a habit merely
Of fingering change – but still Van Horne went on
To clinch his case: the north shore could avoid
The over-border route – a national point
If ever there was one. He promised this
As soon as he was through with buffalo-grass.
And then the little matter of the Rockies:
This must be swallowed without argument,
As obvious as space, clear as a charter.
But why the change in Fleming's survey? Why
The Kicking Horse and not the Yellowhead?
The national point again. The Kicking Horse
Was shorter, closer to the boundary line;
No rival road would build between the two.
He did not dwell upon the other Passes.
He promised all with surety of schedule,
And with a self-imposed serenity
That dried the sweat upon the Board Room faces.

NUMBER ONE

Oak Lake to Calgary. Van Horne took off
His coat. The North must wait, for that would mean
His shirt as well. First and immediate
This prairie pledge–five hundred miles, and it
Was winter. Failure of this trial promise
Would mean–no, it must not be there for meaning.
An order from him carried no repeal:
It was as final as an execution.
A cable started rolling mills in Europe:
A tap of Morse sent hundreds to the bush,
Where axes swung on spruce and the saw sang,
Changing the timber into pyramids
Of poles and sleepers. Clicks, despatches, words,
Like lanterns in a night conductor's hands,
Signalled the wheels: a nod put Shaughnessy
In Montreal: supplies moved on the minute.
Thousands of men and mules and horses slipped
Into their togs and harness night and day.
The grass that fed the buffalo was turned over,
The black alluvial mould laid bare, the bed
Levelled and scraped. As individuals
The men lost their identity; as groups,
As gangs, they massed, divided, subdivided,
Like numerals only–sub-contractors, gangs
Of engineers, and shovel gangs for bridges,
Culverts, gangs of mechanics stringing wires,
Loading, unloading and reloading gangs,
Gangs for the fish-plates and the spiking gangs,
Putting a silver polish on the nails.
But neither men nor horses ganged like mules:
Wiser than both they learned to unionize.
Some instinct in their racial nether regions
Had taught them how to sniff the five-hour stretch
Down to the fine arithmetic of seconds.
They tired out their rivals and they knew it.
They'd stand for overwork, not overtime.
Faster than workmen could fling down their shovels,
They could unhinge their joints, unhitch their tendons;
Jumping the foreman's call, they brayed "*Unhook*"
With a defiant, corporate instancy.
The promise which looked first without redemption
Was being redeemed. From three to seven miles

A day the parallels were being laid,
Though Eastern throats were hoarse with the old question –
Where are the settlements? And whence the gift
Of tongues which could pronounce place-names that purred
Like cats in relaxation after kittens?
Was it a part of the same pledge to turn
A shack into a bank for notes renewed;
To call a site a city when men saw
Only a water-tank? This was an act
Of faith indeed – substance of things unseen –
Which would convert preachers to miracles,
Lure teachers into lean-to's for their classes.
And yet it happened that while labourers
Were swearing at their blisters in the evening
And straightening out their spinal kinks at dawn,
The tracks joined up Oak Lake to Calgary.

NUMBER TWO

On the North Shore a reptile lay asleep –
A hybrid that the myths might have conceived,
But not delivered, as progenitor
Of crawling, gliding things upon the earth.
She lay snug in the folds of a huge boa
Whose tail had covered Labrador and swished
Atlantic tides, whose body coiled itself
Around the Hudson Bay, then curled up north
Through Manitoba and Saskatchewan
To Great Slave Lake. In continental reach
The neck went past the Great Bear Lake until
Its head was hidden in the Arctic Seas.
This folded reptile was asleep or dead:
So motionless, she seemed stone dead – just seemed:
She was too old for death, too old for life,
For as if jealous of all living forms
She had lain there before bivalves began
To catacomb their shells on western mountains.
Somewhere within this life-death zone she sprawled,
Torpid upon a rock-and-mineral mattress.
Ice-ages had passed by and over her,
But these, for all their motion, had but sheared
Her spotty carboniferous hair or made
Her ridges stand out like the spikes of molochs.

Her back grown stronger every million years,
She had shed water by the longer rivers
To Hudson Bay and by the shorter streams
To the great basins to the south, had filled
Them up, would keep them filled until the end
Of Time.

        Was this the thing Van Horne set out
To conquer? When Superior lay there
With its inviting levels? Blake, Mackenzie,
Offered this water like a postulate.
"Why those twelve thousand men sent to the North?
Nonsense and waste with utter bankruptcy."
And the Laurentian monster at the first
Was undisturbed, presenting but her bulk
To the invasion. All she had to do
Was lie there neither yielding nor resisting.
Top-heavy with accumulated power
And overgrown survival without function,
She changed her spots as though brute rudiments
Of feeling foreign to her native hour
Surprised her with a sense of violation
From an existence other than her own –
Or why take notice of this unknown breed,
This horde of bipeds that could toil like ants,
Could wake her up and keep her irritated?
They tickled her with shovels, dug pickaxes
Into her scales and got under her skin,
And potted holes in her with drills and filled
Them up with what looked like fine grains of sand,
Black sand. It wasn't noise that bothered her,
For thunder she was used to from her cradle –
The head-push and nose-blowing of the ice,
The height and pressure of its body: these
Like winds native to clime and habitat
Had served only to lull her drowsing coils.
It was not size or numbers that concerned her.
It was their foreign build, their gait of movement.
They did not crawl – nor were they born with wings.
They stood upright and walked, shouted and sang;
They needed air – that much was true – their mouths
Were open but the tongue was alien.
The sounds were not the voice of winds and waters,
Nor that of any beasts upon the earth.

She took them first with lethargy, suffered
The rubbing of her back – those little jabs
Of steel were like the burrowing of ticks
In an elk's needing an antler point,
Or else left in a numb monotony.
These she could stand but when the breed
Advanced west on her higher vertebrae,
Kicking most insolently at her ribs,
Pouring black powder in her cavities,
And making not the clouds but her insides
The home of fire and thunder, then she gave
Them trial of her strength: the trestles tottered;
Abutments, bridges broke; her rivers flooded:
She summoned snow and ice, and then fell back
On the last weapon in her armoury –
The first and last – her passive corporal bulk,
To stay or wreck the schedule of Van Horne.

NUMBER THREE

The big one was the mountains – seas indeed!
With crests whiter than foam: they poured like seas,
Fluting the green banks of the pines and spruces.
An eagle-flight above they hid themselves
In clouds. They carried space upon their ledges.
Could these be overridden frontally,
Or like typhoons outsmarted on the flanks?
And what were on the flanks? The troughs and canyons,
Passes more dangerous to the navigator
Than to Magellan when he tried to read
The barbarous language of his Strait by calling
For echoes from the rocky hieroglyphs
Playing their pranks of hide-and-seek in fog:
As stubborn too as the old North-West Passage,
More difficult, for ice-packs could break up;
And as for bergs, what polar architect
Could stretch his compass points to draught such peaks
As kept on rising there beyond the foothills?
And should the bastions of the Rockies yield
To this new human and unnatural foe,
Would not the Selkirks stand? This was a range
That looked like some strange dread outside a door
Which gave its name but would not show its features,

Leaving them to the mind to guess at. This
Meant tunnels – would there be no end to boring?
There must be some day. Fleming and his men
Had nosed their paths like hounds; but paths and trails,
Measured in every inch by chain and transit,
Looked easy and seductive on a chart.
The rivers out there did not flow: they tumbled.
The cataracts were fed by glaciers;
Eddies were thought as whirlpools in the Gorges,
And gradients had paws that tore up tracks.

Terror and beauty like twin signal flags
Flew on the peaks for men to keep their distance.
The two combined as in a storm at sea –
"Stay on the shore and take your fill of breathing,
But come not to the decks and climb the rigging."
The Ranges could put cramps in hands and feet
Merely by the suggestion of the venture.
They needed miles to render up their beauty,
As if the gods in high aesthetic moments,
Resenting the profanity of touch,
Chiselled this sculpture for the eye alone.

(*Van Horne in momentary meditation at the Foothills.*)

His name was now a legend. The North Shore,
Though not yet conquered, yet had proved that he
Could straighten crooked roads by pulling at them,
Shear down a hill and drain a bog or fill
A valley overnight. Fast as a bobcat,
He'd climb and run across the shakiest trestle
Or, with a locomotive short of coal,
He could supply the head of steam himself.
He breakfasted on bridges, lunched on ties;
Drinking from gallon pails, he dined on moose.
He could tire out the lumberjacks; beat hell
From workers but no more than from himself.
Only the devil or Paul Bunyan shared
With him the secret of perpetual motion,
And when he moved among his men they looked
For shoulder sprouts upon the Flying Dutchman.

But would his legend crack upon the mountains?
There must be no retreat: his bugles knew
Only one call – the summons to advance
Against two fortresses: the mind, the rock.
To prove the first defence was vulnerable,
To tap the treasury at home and then
Untie the purse-strings of the Londoners,
As hard to loosen as salt-water knots –
That job was Stephen's, Smith's, Tupper's, Macdonald's.
He knew its weight: had heard, as well as they,
Blake pumping at his pulmonary bellows,
And if the speeches made the House shock-proof
Before they ended, they could still peal forth
From print more durable than spoken tones.
Blake had returned to the attack and given
Sir John the ague with another phrase
As round and as melodious as the first:
*"The Country's wealth, its millions after millions
Squandered* – LOST IN THE GORGES OF THE FRASER":
A beautiful but ruinous piece of music
That could only be drowned with drums and fifes.
Tupper, fighting with fists and nails and toes,
Had taken the word *scandal* which had cut
His master's ballots, and had turned the edge
With his word *slander*, but Blake's *sea*, how turn
That edge? Now this last devastating phrase!
But let Sir John and Stephen answer this
Their way. Van Horne must answer it in his.

INTERNECINE STRIFE

The men were fighting foes which had themselves
Waged elemental civil wars and still
Were hammering one another at this moment.
The peaks and ranges flung from ocean beds
Had wakened up one geologic morning
To find their scalps raked off, their lips punched in,
The colour of their skins charged with new dyes.
Some of them did not wake or but half-woke;
Prone or recumbent with the eerie shapes
Of creatures that would follow them. Weather
Had acted on their spines and frozen them
To stegosaurs or, taking longer cycles,

Divining human features, had blown back
Their hair and, pressing on their cheeks and temples,
Bestowed on them the gravity of mummies.
But there was life and power which belied
The tombs. Guerrilla evergreens were climbing
In military order: at the base
The *ponderosa* pine; the fir backed up
The spruce; and it the Stoney Indian lodge-poles;
And these the white-barks; then, deciduous,
The outpost suicidal Lyell larches
Aiming at summits, digging scraggy roots
Around the boulders in the thinning soil,
Till they were stopped dead at the timber limit –
Rock *versus* forest with the rock prevailing.
Or with the summer warmth it was the ice,
In treaty with the rock to hold a line
As stubborn as a Balkan boundary,
That left its caves to score the Douglases,
And smother them with half a mile of dirt,
And making snow-sheds, covering the camps,
Futile as parasols in polar storms.
One enemy alone had battled rock
And triumphed: searching levels like lost broods,
Keen on their ocean scent, the rivers cut
The quartzite, licked the slate and softened it,
Till mud solidified was mud again,
And then, digesting it like earthworms, squirmed
Along the furrows with one steering urge –
To navigate the mountains in due time
Back to their home in worm-casts on the tides.

Into this scrimmage came the fighting men,
And all but rivers were their enemies.
Whether alive or dead the bush resisted:
Alive, it must be slain with axe and saw,
If dead, it was in tangle at their feet.
The ice could hit men as it hit the spruces.
Even the rivers had betraying tricks,
Watched like professed allies across a border.
They smiled from fertile plains and easy runs
Of valley gradients: their eyes got narrow,
Full of suspicion at the gorges where
They leaped and put the rickets in the trestles.
Though natively in conflict with the rock,

Both leagued against invasion. At Hell's Gate
A mountain laboured and brought forth a bull
Which, stranded in mid-stream, was fighting back
The river, and the fight turned on the men,
Demanding from this route their bread and steel.
And there below the Gate was the Black Canyon
With twenty-miles-an-hour burst of speed.

(ONDERDONK BUILDS THE "SKUZZY" TO FORCE THE PASSAGE.)

Twas more than navigation: only eagles
Might follow up this run; the spawning salmon
Gulled by the mill-race had returned to rot
Their upturned bellies in the canyon eddies.
Two engines at the stern, a forrard winch,
Steam-powered, failed to stem the cataract.
The last resource was shoulders, arms and hands.
Fifteen men at the capstan, creaking hawsers,
Two hundred Chinese tugging at shore ropes
To keep her bow-on from the broadside drift,
The *Skuzzy* under steam and muscle took
The shoals and rapids, and warped through the Gate,
Until she reached the navigable water—
The adventure was not sailing: it was climbing.

As hard a challenge were the precipices
Worn water-smooth and sheer a thousand feet.
Surveyors from the edges looked for footholds,
But, finding none, they tried marine manoeuvres.
Out of a hundred men they drafted sailors
Whose toes as supple as their fingers knew
The wash of reeling decks, whose knees were hardened
Through tying gaskets at the royal yards:
They lowered them with knotted ropes and drew them
Along the face until the lines were strung
Between the juts. Barefooted, dynamite
Strapped to their waists, the sappers followed, treading
The spider films and chipping holes for blasts,
Until the cliffs delivered up their features
Under the civil discipline of roads.

RING, RING THE BELLS

Ring, ring the bells, but not the engine bells:
Today only the ritual of the steeple
Chanted to the dull tempo of the toll.
Sorrow is stalking through the camps, speaking
A common mother-tongue. 'Twill leave tomorrow
To turn that language on a Blackfoot tepee,
Then take its leisurely Pacific time
To tap its fingers on a coolie's door.
Ring, ring the bells but not the engine bells:
Today only that universal toll,
For granite, mixing dust with human lime,
Had so compounded bodies into boulders
As to untype the blood, and, then, the Fraser,
Catching the fragments from the dynamite,
Had bleached all birthmarks from her swirling dead.

Tomorrow and the engine bells again!

THE LAKE OF MONEY

(The appeal to the Government for a loan of
twenty-two-and-a-half million, 1883.)

Sir John began to muse on his excuses.
Was there no bottom to this lake? One mile
Along that northern strip had cost – how much?
Eleven dollars to the inch. The Road
In all would measure up to ninety millions,
And diverse hands were plucking at his elbow.
The Irish and the Dutch he could outface,
Outquip. He knew Van Horne and Shaughnessy
Had little time for speeches – one was busy
In grinding out two thousand miles; the other
Was working wizardry on creditors,
Pulling rabbits from hats, gold coins from sleeves
In Montreal. As for his foes like Blake,
He thanked his household gods the Irishman
Could claim only a viscous brand of humour,
Heavy, impenetrable till the hour
To laugh had taken on a chestnut colour.
But Stephen was his friend, hard to resist.

And there was Smith. He knew that both had pledged
Their private fortunes as security
For the construction of the Road. But that
Was not enough. Sir John had yet to dip
And scrape farther into the public pocket,
Explore its linings: his, the greater task;
His, to commit a nation to the risk.
How could he face the House with pauper hands?
He had to deal with Stephen first – a man
Laconic, nailing points and clinching them.
Oratory, the weapon of the massed assemblies
Was not the weapon here – Scot meeting Scot.
The burr was hard to take; and Stephen had
A Banffshire-cradled *r*. Drilling the ear,
It paralysed the nerves, hit the red cells.
The logic in the sound, escaping print,
Would seep through channels and befog the cortex.

Sir John counted the exits of discretion:
Disguise himself? A tailor might do much;
A barber might trim down his mane, brush back
The forelock, but no artist of massage,
Kneading that face from brow to nasal tip,
Could change a chunk of granite into talc.
His rheumatism? Yet he still could walk.
Neuralgia did not interfere with speech.
The bronchial tubing needed softer air?
Vacations could not cancel all appointments.
Men saw him in the flesh at Ottawa.
He had to speak this week, wheedling committees,
Much easier than to face a draper's clerk,
Tongue-trained on Aberdonian bargain-counters.
He raised his closed left hand to straighten out
His fingers one by one – four million people.
He had to pull a trifle on that fourth,
Not so resilient as the other three.
Only a wrench could stir the little finger
Which answered with a vicious backward jerk.

The dollar fringes of one hundred million
Were smirching up the blackboard of his mind.
But curving round and through them was the thought
He could not sponge away. Had he not fathered
The Union? Prodigy indeed it was
From Coast to Coast. Was not the Line essential?
What was this fungus sprouting from his rind
That left him at the root less clear a growth
Than this Dutch immigrant, William Van Horne?
The name suggested artificial land
Rescued from swamp by bulging dikes and ditches;
And added now to that were bogs and sloughs
And that most cursèd diabase which God
Had left from the explosions of his wrath.
And yet this man was challenging his pride.
North-Sea ancestral moisture on his beard,
Van Horne was now the spokesman for the West,
The champion of an all-Canadian route,
The Yankee who had come straight over, linked
His name and life with the Canadian nation.
Besides, he had infected the whole camp.
Whether acquired or natural, the stamp
Of faith had never left his face. Was it
The artist's instinct which had made the Rockies
And thence the Selkirks, scenes of tourist lure,
As easy for the passage of an engine
As for the flight of eagles? Miracles
Became his thought: the others took their cue
From him. They read the lines upon his lips.
But miracles did not spring out of air.
Under the driving will and sweltering flesh
They came from pay-cars loaded with the cash.
So that was why Stephen had called so often –
Money – that lake of money, bonds, more bonds.

(*The Bill authorizing the loan stubbornly carries
the House.*)

DYNAMITE ON THE NORTH SHORE

The lizard was in sanguinary mood.
She had been waked again: she felt her sleep
Had lasted a few seconds of her time.
The insects had come back – the ants, if ants
They were – dragging *those* trees, *those* logs athwart
Her levels, driving in *those* spikes; and how
The long grey snakes unknown within her region
Wormed from the east, unstripped, sunning themselves
Uncoiled upon the logs and then moved on,
Growing each day, ever keeping abreast!
She watched them, waiting for a bloody moment,
Until the borers halted at a spot,
The most invulnerable of her whole column,
Drove in that iron, wrenched it in the holes,
Hitting, digging, twisting. Why that spot?
Not this the former itch. That sharp proboscis
Was out for more than self-sufficing blood
About the cuticle: 'twas out for business
In the deep layers and the arteries.
And this consistent punching at her belly
With fire and thunder slapped her like an insult,
As with the blasts the caches of her broods
Broke – nickel, copper, silver and fool's gold,
Burst from their immemorial dormitories
To sprawl indecent in the light of day.
Another warning – this time different.

Westward above her webs she had a trap –
A thing called muskeg, easy on the eyes
Stung with the dust of gravel. Cotton grass,
Its white spires blending with the orchids,
Peeked through green table-cloths of sphagnum moss.
Carnivorous bladder-wort studded the acres,
Passing the water-fleas through their digestion.
Sweet-gale and sundew edged the dwarf black spruce;
And herds of cariboo had left their hoof-marks,
Betraying visual solidity,
But like the thousands of the pitcher plants,
Their downward-pointing hairs alluring insects,
Deceptive – and the men were moving west!
Now was her time. She took three engines, sank them
With seven tracks down through the hidden lake

To the rock bed, then over them she spread
A counterpane of leather-leaf and slime.
A warning, that was all for now. 'Twas sleep
She wanted, sleep, for drowsing was her pastime
And waiting through eternities of seasons.
As for intruders bred for skeletons –
Some day perhaps when ice began to move,
Or some convulsion ran fires through her tombs,
She might stir in her sleep and far below
The reach of steel and blast of dynamite,
She'd claim their bones as her possessive right
And wrap them cold in her pre-Cambrian folds.

THREATS OF SECESSION

The Lady's face was flushed. Thirteen years now
Since that engagement ring adorned her finger!
Adorned? Betrayed. She often took it off
And flung it angrily upon the dresser,
Then took excursions with her sailor-lover.
Had that man with a throat like Ottawa,
That tailored suitor in a cut-away,
Presumed compliance on her part? High time
To snub him for delay – for was not time
The marrow of agreement? At the mirror
She tried to cream a wrinkle from her forehead,
Toyed with the ring, replaced it and removed it.
Harder, she thought, to get it on and off –
This like the wrinkle meant but one thing, age.
So not too fast; play safe. Perhaps the man
Was not the master of his choice. Someone
Within the family group might well contest
Exotic marriage. Still, her plumes were ruffled
By Blake's two-nights' address before the Commons:
Three lines inside the twenty-thousand words
Had maddened her. She searched for hidden meanings –
*"Should she insist on those preposterous terms
And threaten to secede, then let her go,
Better than ruin the country."* "Let her go,"
And *"ruin"* – language this to shake her bodice.
Was this indictment of her character,
Or worse, her charm? Or was it just plain dowry?
For this last one at least she had an answer.

Pay now or separation – this the threat.
Dipping the ring into a soapy lather,
She pushed it to the second knuckle, twirled
It past. Although the diamond was off-colour,
She would await its partner ring of gold –
The finest carat; yes, by San Francisco!

BACK TO THE MOUNTAINS

As grim an enemy as rock was time.
The little men from five-to-six feet high,
From three-to-four score years in lease of breath,
Were flung in double-front against them both
In years a billion strong; so long was it
Since brachiapods in mollusc habitats
Were clamping shells on weed in ocean mud.
Now only yesterday had Fleming's men,
Searching for toeholds on the sides of cliffs,
Five thousand feet above sea-level, set
A tripod's leg upon a trilobite.
And age meant pressure, density. Sullen
With aeons, mountains would not stand aside;
Just block the path – morose but without anger,
No feeling in the menace of their frowns,
Immobile for they had no need of motion;
Their veins possessed no blood – they carried quartzite.
Frontal assault! To go through them direct
Seemed just as inconceivable as ride
Over their peaks. But go through them the men
Were ordered and their weapons were their hands
And backs, pickaxes, shovels, hammers, drills
And dynamite – against the rock and time;
For here the labour must be counted up
In months subject to clauses of a contract
Distinguished from the mortgage-run an age
Conceded to the trickle of the rain
In building river-homes. The men bored in,
The mesozoic rock arguing the inches.

This was a kind of surgery unknown
To mountains or the mothers of the myths.
These had a chloroform in leisured time,
Squeezing a swollen handful of light-seconds,

When water like a wriggling casuist
Had probed and found the areas for incision.
Now time was rushing labour – inches grew
To feet, to yards; the drills – the single jacks,
The double jacks – drove in and down; the holes
Gave way to excavations, these to tunnels,
Till men sodden with mud and roof-drip steamed
From sunlight through the tar-black to the sunlight.

HOLLOW ECHOES FROM THE TREASURY VAULT

Sir John was tired as to the point of death.
His chin was anchored to his chest. Was Blake
Right after all? And was Mackenzie right?
Superior could be travelled on. Besides,
It had a bottom, but those northern bogs
Like quicksands could go down to the earth's core.
Compared with them, quagmires of ancient legend
Were backyard puddles for old ducks. To sink
Those added millions down that wallowing hole!
He thought now through his feet. Many a time
When argument cemented opposition,
And hopeless seemed his case, he could think up
A tale to laugh the benches to accord.
No one knew better, when a point had failed
The brain, how to divert it through the ribs.
But now his stock of stories had run out.
This was exhaustion at its coma level.
Or was he sick? Never had spots like these
Assailed his eyes. He could not rub them out –
Those shifting images – was it the sunset
Refracted through the bevelled window edges?
He shambled over and drew down the blind;
Returned and slumped; it was no use; the spots
Were there. No light could ever shoot this kind
Of orange through a prism, or this blue,
And what a green! The spectrum was ruled out;
Its bands were too inviolate. He rubbed
The lids again – a brilliant gold appeared
Upon a silken backdrop of pure white,
And in the centre, red – a scarlet red,
A dancing, rampant and rebellious red
That like a strain spread outward covering

The vision field. He closed his eyes and listened:
Why, what was that? 'Twas bad enough that light
Should play such pranks upon him, but must sound
Crash the Satanic game, reverberate
A shot fifteen years after it was fired,
And culminate its echoes with the thud
Of marching choruses outside his window:

"We'll hang Riel up the Red River,
And he'll roast in hell forever,
We'll hang him up the River
With a yah-yah-yah."

The noose was for the shot: 'twas blood for blood;
The death of Riel for the death of Scott.
What could not Blake do with that on the Floor,
Or that young, tall, bilingual advocate
Who with the carriage of his syllables
Could bid an audience like an orchestra
Answer his body swaying like a reed?
Colours and sounds made riot of his mind –
White horses in July processional prance,
The blackrobe's swish, the Métis' sullen tread,
And out there in the rear the treaty-wise
Full-breeds with buffalo wallows on their foreheads.

This he could stand no longer, sick indeed:
Send for his doctor, the first thought, then No;
The doctor would advise an oculist,
The oculist return him to the doctor.
The doctor would see-saw him to another –
A specialist on tumours of the brain,
And he might recommend close-guarded rest
In some asylum – Devil take them all,
He had his work to do. He glanced about
And spied his medicine upon the sideboard;
Amber it was, distilled from Highland springs,
That often had translated age to youth
And boiled his blood on a victorious rostrum.
Conviction seized him as he stood, for here
At least he was not cut for compromise,
Nor curried to his nickname Old Tomorrow.
Deliberation in his open stance,
He trenched a deep one, gurgled and sat down.

What were those paltry millions after all?
They stood between completion of the Road
And bankruptcy of both Road and Nation.
Those north-shore gaps must be closed in by steel.
It did not need exhilarated judgment
To see the sense of that. To send the men
Hop-skip-and-jump upon lake ice to board
The flatcars was a revelry for imps.
And all that cutting through the mountain rock,
Four years of it and more, and all for nothing,
Unless those gaps were spanned, bedded and railed.
To quit the Road, to have the Union broken
Was irredeemable. He rose, this time
Invincibility carved on his features,
Hoisted a second, then drew up the blind.
He never saw a sunset just like this.
He lingered in the posture of devotion:
That sun for sure was in the west, or was it?
Soon it would be upholstering the clouds
Upon the Prairies, Rockies and the Coast:
He turned and sailed back under double-reef,
Cabined himself inside an armchair, stretched
His legs to their full length under the table.
Something miraculous had changed the air –
A chemistry that knew how to extract
The iron from the will: the spots had vanished
And in their place an unterrestrial nimbus
Circled his hair: the jerks had left his nerves:
The millions kept on shrinking or were running
From right to left: the fourth arthritic digit
Was straight, and yes, by heaven, the little fifth
Which up to now was just a calcium hook
Was suppling in the Hebridean warmth.
A blessèd peace fell like a dew upon him,
And soon, in trance, drenched in conciliation,
He hiccupped gently – *"Now let S-S-Stephen come!"*

*(The Government grants the Directors the right
to issue $35,000,000, guarantees $20,000,000, the
rest to be issued by the Railway Directors.
Stephen goes to London, and Lord Revelstoke,
speaking for the House of Baring, takes over the
issue.)*

SUSPENSE IN THE MONTREAL BOARD ROOM

Evening had settled hours before its time
Within the Room and on the face of Angus.
Dejection overlaid his social fur,
Rumpled his side-burns, left moustache untrimmed.
The vision of his Bank, his future Shops,
Was like his outlook for the London visit.
Van Horne was fronting him with a like visage
Except for two spots glowing on his cheeks –
Dismay and anger at those empty pay-cars.
His mutterings were indistinct but final
As though he were reciting to himself
The Athanasian damnatory clauses.
He felt the Receiver's breath upon his neck:
To come so near the end, and then this hurdle!

Only one thing could penetrate that murk –
A cable pledge from London, would it come?
Till now refusal or indifference
Had met the overtures. Would Stephen turn
The trick?
          A door-knock and a telegram
With Stephen's signature! Van Horne ripped it
Apart. Articulation failed his tongue,
But Angus got the meaning from his face
And from a noisy sequence of deductions: –
An inkstand coasted through the office window,
Followed by shredded maps and blotting-pads,
Fluttering like shad-flies in a summer gale;
A bookshelf smitten by a fist collapsed;
Two chairs flew to the ceiling – one retired,
The other roosted on the chandelier.
Some thirty years erased like blackboard chalk,
Van Horne was in a school at Illinois.
Triumphant over his two-hundred weight,
He leaped and turned a cartwheel on the table,
Driving heel sparables into the oak,
Came down to teach his partner a Dutch dance;
And in the presence of the messenger,
Who stared immobilized at what he thought
New colours in the managerial picture,
Van Horne took hold of Angus bodily,

Tore off his tie and collar, mauled his shirt,
And stuffed a Grand Trunk folder down his breeches.

(*The last gap in the mountain – between the*
Selkirks and Savona's Ferry – is closed.)

The Road itself was like a stream that men
Had coaxed and teased or bullied out of Nature.
As if watching for weak spots in her codes,
It sought for levels like the watercourses.
It sinuously took the bends, rejoiced
In plains and easy grades, found gaps, poured through them,
But hating steep descents avoided them.
Unlike the rivers which in full rebellion
Against the canyons' hydrophobic slaver
Went to the limit of their argument:
Unlike again, the stream of steel had found
A way to climb, became a mountaineer.
From the Alberta plains it reached the Summit,
And where it could not climb, it cut and curved,
Till from the Rockies to the Coastal Range
It had accomplished what the Rivers had,
Making a hundred clean Caesarian cuts,
And bringing to delivery in their time
Their smoky, lusty-screaming locomotives.

THE SPIKE

Silver or gold? Van Horne had rumbled "*Iron*".
No flags or bands announced this ceremony,
No Morse in circulation through the world,
And though the vital words like Eagle Pass,
Craigellachie, were trembling in their belfries,
No hands were at the ropes. The air was taut
With silences as rigid as the spruces
Forming the background in November mist.
More casual than camera-wise, the men
Could have been properties upon a stage,
Except for road maps furrowing their faces.

Rogers, his both feet planted on a tie,
Stood motionless as ballast. In the rear,
Covering the scene with spirit-level eyes,

Predestination on his chin, was Fleming.
The only one groomed for the ritual
From smooth silk hat and well-cut square-rig beard
Down through his Caledonian longitude,
He was outstaturing others by a foot,
And upright as the mainmast of a brig.
Beside him, barely reaching to his waist,
A water-boy had wormed his way in front
To touch this rail with his foot, his face
Upturned to see the cheek-bone crags of Rogers.
The other side of Fleming, hands in pockets,
Eyes leaden-lidded under square-crowned hat,
And puncheon-bellied under overcoat,
Unsmiling at the focused lens – Van Horne.
Whatever ecstasy played round that rail
Did not leap to his face. Five years had passed,
Less than five years – so well within the pledge.

The job was done. Was this the slouch of rest?
Not to the men he drove through walls of granite.
The embers from the past were in his soul,
Banked for the moment at the rail and smoking,
Just waiting for the future to be blown.

At last the spike and Donald with the hammer!
His hair like frozen moss from Labrador
Poked out under his hat, ran down his face
To merge with streaks of rust in a white cloud.
What made him fumble the first stroke? Not age:
The snow belied his middle sixties. Was
It lapse of caution or his sense of thrift,
That elemental stuff which through his life
Never pockmarked his daring but had made
The man the canniest trader of his time,
Who never missed a rat-count, never failed
To gauge the size and texture of a pelt?
Now here he was caught by the camera,
Back bent, head bowed, and staring at a sledge,
Outwitted by an idiotic nail.
Though from the crowd no laughter, yet the spike
With its slewed neck was grinning up at Smith.

*   *   *

Wrenched out, it was replaced. This time the hammer
Gave a first tap as with apology,
Another one, another, till the spike
Was safely stationed in the tie and then
The Scot, invoking his ancestral clan,
Using the hammer like a battle-axe,
His eyes bloodshot with memories of Flodden,
Descended on it, rammed it to its home.

      *   *   *

The stroke released a trigger for a burst
Of sound that stretched the gamut of the air.
The shouts of engineers and dynamiters,
Of locomotive-workers and explorers,
Flanking the rails, were but a tuning-up
For a massed continental chorus. Led
By Moberly (of the Eagles and *this* Pass)
And Rogers (of *his own*), followed by Wilson,
And Ross (charged with the Rocky Mountain Section),
By Egan (general of the Western Lines),
Cambie and Marcus Smith, Harris of Boston,
The roar was deepened by the bass of Fleming,
And heightened by the laryngeal fifes
Of Dug McKenzie and John H. McTavish.
It ended when Van Horne spat out some phlegm
To ratify the tumult with "*Well Done*"
Tied in a knot of monosyllables.

Merely the tuning up! For on the morrow
The last blow on the spike would stir the mould
Under the drumming of the prairie wheels,
And make the whistles from the steam out-crow
The Fraser. Like a gavel it would close
Debate, making Macdonald's "*sea to sea*"
Pour through two oceanic megaphones –
Three thousand miles of *Hail* from port to port;
And somewhere in the middle of the line
Of steel, even the lizard heard the stroke.
The breed had triumphed after all. To drown
The traffic chorus, she must blend the sound
With those inaugural, narcotic notes
Of storm and thunder which would send her back
Deeper than ever in Laurentian sleep.

F. R.
SCOTT

F. R. Scott was born in Quebec City in 1899, the son of an Anglican clergyman who was soon to become a Canon of the Cathedral and who had already published some books of poetry. He received a B.A. from Bishop's University in 1919, was appointed a Rhodes Scholar from the Province of Quebec, and read history at Magdalen College, Oxford. He returned to Canada in 1923 and, after a brief spell as a schoolmaster, decided to study law in the McGill Graduate School. Scott joined the McGill Law Faculty in 1928 and his academic career as a Professor of Constitutional Law led to his ultimately becoming Dean of the Faculty, a post from which he retired in 1965. His career as a lawyer has involved the active defence of specific minority rights as well as the study of constitutional and legislative problems of a more technical and general nature. His political activities have ranged from active assistance in the early days of the CCF Party (he helped to draw up the Regina Manifesto of 1933) to being United Nations Technical Assistance Resident Representative in Burma in 1952. He has published many articles on civil rights cases, on Confederation and the Constitution, and on the British Commonwealth. His editing (and contributing to) collections like *Planning for Canada* (1935) and *Make This Your Canada* (1943) are part of that concern for an improved social order which led to his work for the CCF.

As a graduate student Scott printed poems in the new *McGill Fortnightly Review*, which he helped to found in 1925. After it died, he helped to found the short-lived *Canadian Mercury* of 1928. Many of his early poems were rather austere, imagistic pieces, while others were satirical attacks on social, political, educational, and literary targets. In the thirties such poems continued to appear in *The Canadian Forum* and Scott, like Smith, was one of the six poets included in *New Provinces* (Macmillan, 1936). He did not publish a separate volume, however, until *Overture* (Ryerson, 1945). It has been succeeded by *Events and Signals* (Ryerson, 1954), *The Eye of the Needle* (Contact Press, 1957), *Signature* (Klanak Press, 1964) and *Selected Poems* (Oxford, 1966). He has also published translations of French-Canadian poetry. His readers and critics have been inclined to agree that Scott shows many of the advantages of being a wide-ranging and committed human being first and a poet second, and only a few of the disadvantages. The public and humane man seems to join forces with the private and demanding craftsman.

The Canadian Authors Meet

Expansive puppets percolate self-unction
Beneath a portrait of the Prince of Wales.
Miss Crotchet's muse has somehow failed to function,
Yet she's a poetess. Beaming, she sails

From group to chattering group, with such a dear
Victorian saintliness, as is her fashion,
Greeting the other unknowns with a cheer —
Virgins of sixty who still write of passion.

The air is heavy with Canadian topics,
And Carman, Lampman, Roberts, Campbell, Scott,
Are measured for their faith and philanthropics,
Their zeal for God and King, their earnest thought.

The cakes are sweet, but sweeter is the feeling
That one is mixing with the *literati*;
It warms the old, and melts the most congealing.
Really, it is a most delightful party.

Shall we go round the mulberry bush, or shall
We gather at the river, or shall we
Appoint a Poet Laureate this fall,
Or shall we have another cup of tea?

O Canada, O Canada, Oh can
A day go by without new authors springing
To paint the native maple, and to plan
More ways to set the selfsame welkin ringing?

Overture

In the dark room, under a cone of light,
You precisely play the Mozart sonata. The bright
Clear notes fly like sparks through the air
And trace a flickering pattern of music there.

Your hands dart in the light, your fingers flow.
They are ten careful operatives in a row
That pick their packets of sound from steel bars
Constructing harmonies as sharp as stars.

But how shall I hear old music? This is an hour
Of new beginnings, concepts warring for power,
Decay of systems—the tissue of art is torn
With overtures of an era being born.

And this perfection which is less yourself
Than Mozart, seems a trinket on a shelf,
A pretty octave played before a window
Beyond whose curtain grows a world crescendo.

Summer Camp

Here is a lovely little camp
Built among the Laurentian hills
By a Children's Welfare Society,
Which is entirely supported by voluntary contributions.
All summer long underprivileged children scamper about
And it is astonishing how soon they look happy and well.
Two weeks here in the sun and air
Through the charity of our wealthy citizens
Will be a wonderful help to the little tots
When they return for a winter in the slums.

Efficiency: 1935

The efficiency of the capitalist system
Is rightly admired by important people.
Our huge steel mills
Operating at 25% of capacity
Are the last word in organization.
The new grain elevators
Stored with superfluous wheat
Can load a grain-boat in two hours.
Marvellous card-sorting machines
Make it easy to keep track of the unemployed.
There is not one unnecessary worker
In these textile plants
That require a 75% tariff protection.
And when our closed shoe-factories re-open
They will produce more footwear than we can possibly buy.
So don't let us start experimenting with socialism
Which everyone knows means inefficiency and waste.

Old Song

far voices
and fretting leaves
this music the
hillside gives

but in the deep
Laurentian river
an elemental song
for ever

a quiet calling
of no mind
out of long æons
when dust was blind
and ice hid sound

only a moving
with no note
granite lips
a stone throat

North Stream

Ice mothers me
My bed is rock
Over sand I move silently.

I am crystal clear
To a sunbeam.
No grasses grow in me
My banks are clean.

Foam runs from the rapid
To rest on my dark pools.

Abstract

Sharply place a cube edgewise
By a still, dark water.

Let the tall cone float on a disk of stone.

Peel bark from trees so broken stems can stare
At the winged skeleton of the extinct bird
Poised, angular, over the moon-bright rock.

Devoir Molluscule

Make small and hard,
Make round, distinct and hard
These verities that hammer and intrude
Upon the careless fringes of the soul.
O leave not these sharp grains
Without their shell of lustre and allure.

Advice

Beware the casual need
By which the heart is bound;
Pluck out the quickening seed
That falls on stony ground.

Forgo the shallow gain,
The favour of an hour.
Escape, by early pain,
The death before the flower.

Hardest It Is

Your touch is a torch,
A bruise, the spirit broken,
Slow movement under an arch,
The sea's interminable motion.

Contact slackens, too long extended,
Contact quickens, infinitely withheld.
Between hard and harder lies the ecstasy.
Hardest it is to touch yet have and hold.

Ode to a Politician

Item: A STURDY BOY

In simple cottage, with scant ceremonial,
Observe the birthday of this young colonial.

Clutching the nearest good as best he can
The helpless mite perceives no social plan.

He grows unhampered in his natural skills
And finds companionship in lakes and hills.

Item: A FORKED ROAD

But soon this native freedom meets its end
And his fresh mind to ancient rules must bend.

At school he learns the three Canadian things:
Obedience, Loyalty, and Love of Kings.

To serve a country other than his own
Becomes for him the highest duty known,

To keep antiquity alive forever
The proper object of his young endeavour.

Item: A YOUNG MAN'S COUNTRY

Hence though the Northland calls him to be free
He never sheds this first servility.

His keen ambition, after several knocks,
Soon finds an outlet in the orthodox.

He does not recognize the new frontiers
Which beckon, as of old, for pioneers.

So he is proud, not seeing the distant star,
To hitch his wagon to the CPR.

Item: DOING WELL

No matter if his income starts from scratch:
In this career he quickly strikes a match.

Proceeding on two rails that never meet
He lands eventually on easy street.

For not a miner digs or farmer sows
Unless to this steel fist some tribute flows.

Item: DOING GOOD

Now full success has brought him wealth and ease
With lots of honorary LL.D.'s.

From this advantage point, still hale and hearty,
He ties his fortune to the Tory Party.

And in return for this attractive feeder
The party promptly choose him as leader.

The public follow at the next election;
So there he reigns – the national selection.

Item: MORE BUSINESS IN GOVERNMENT

Canadians now have picked to run their state
The sort of man who "made their country great."

Once in the saddle, swift the whip he cracks.
The Mounties spring like thistles in his tracks.

When fools complain, or some poor victims squeal,
He meets their protest with an iron heel.

A simple rule for markets he discovers:
To close his own and blast his way to others.

To keep our credit good and money sound
Some novel democratic ways are found.

The rich are paid by taxes on the poor;
The unemployed are chased from door to door;

The wages fall though dividends are earned,
And people starve though surplus food is burned.

Item: A FLICKER OF DOUBT

This chaos kept alive by penal laws
In time gives even our politician pause.

Some glimmering concept of a juster state
Begins to trouble him – but just too late.

His whole life work had dug the grave too deep
In which the people's hopes and fortunes sleep.

Item: AN EPITAPH

To make the single meaning doubly clear
He ends the journey – as a British peer.

Lakeshore

The lake is sharp along the shore
Trimming the bevelled edge of land
To level curves; the fretted sands
Go slanting down through liquid air
Till stones below shift here and there
Floating upon their broken sky
All netted by the prism wave
And rippled where the currents are.

I stare through windows at this cave
Where fish, like planes, slow-motioned, fly.
Poised in a still of gravity
The narrow minnow, flicking fin,
Hangs in a paler, ochre sun,
His doorways open everywhere.

And I am a tall frond that waves
Its head below its rooted feet
Seeking the light that draws it down
To forest floors beyond its reach
Vivid with gloom and eerie dreams.

The water's deepest colonnades
Contract the blood, and to this home
That stirs the dark amphibian
With me the naked swimmers come
Drawn to their prehistoric womb.

They too are liquid as they fall
Like tumbled water loosed above
Until they lie, diagonal,
Within the cool and sheltered grove
Stroked by the fingertips of love.

Silent, our sport is drowned in fact
Too virginal for speech or sound
And each is personal and laned
Along his private aqueduct.

Too soon the tether of the lungs
Is taut and straining, and we rise
Upon our undeveloped wings
Toward the prison of our ground
A secret anguish in our thighs
And mermaids in our memories.

This is our talent, to have grown
Upright in posture, false-erect,
A landed gentry, circumspect,
Tied to a horizontal soil
The floor and ceiling of the soul;
Striving, with cold and fishy care
To make an ocean of the air.

Sometimes, upon a crowded street,
I feel the sudden rain come down
And in the old, magnetic sound
I hear the opening of a gate
That loosens all the seven seas.
Watching the whole creation drown
I muse, alone, on Ararat.

Laurentian Shield

Hidden in wonder and snow, or sudden with summer,
This land stares at the sun in a huge silence
Endlessly repeating something we cannot hear.
Inarticulate, arctic,
Not written on by history, empty as paper,
It leans away from the world with songs in its lakes
Older than love, and lost in the miles.

This waiting is wanting.
It will choose its language
When it has chosen its technic,
A tongue to shape the vowels of its productivity.

A language of flesh and of roses.

Now there are pre-words,
Cabin syllables,
Nouns of settlement
Slowly forming, with steel syntax,
The long sentence of its exploitation.

The first cry was the hunter, hungry for fur,
And the digger for gold, nomad, no-man, a particle;
Then the bold commands of monopoly, big with machines,
Carving its kingdoms out of the public wealth;
And now the drone of the plane, scouting the ice,
Fills all the emptiness with neighbourhood
And links our future over the vanished pole.

But a deeper note is sounding, heard in the mines,
The scattered camps and the mills, a language of life,
And what will be written in the full culture of occupation
Will come, presently, tomorrow,
From millions whose hands can turn this rock into children.

A l'ange avantgardien

We must leave the handrails and the Ariadne-threads,
The psychiatrists and all the apron strings
And take a whole new country for our own.

Of course we are neurotic; we are everything.
Guilt is the backstage of our innocent play.
To us normal and abnormal are two sides of a road.

We shall not fare too well on this journey.
Our food and shelter are not easy to find
In the *salons des réfusés*, the little mags of our friends.

But it is you, rebellious angel, you we trust.
Astride the cultures, feet planted in heaven and hell,
You guard the making, never what's made and paid.

Poetry

Nothing can take its place. If I write "ostrich"
Those who have never seen the bird see it
With its head in the sand and its plumes fluffed with the wind
Like Mackenzie King talking on Freedom of Trade.

And if I write "holocaust", and "nightingales",
I startle the insurance agents and the virgins
Who belong, by this alchemy, in the same category,
Since both are very worried about their premiums.

A rose and a rose are two roses; a rose is a rose is a rose.
Sometimes I have walked down a street marked No Outlet
Only to find that what was blocking my path
Was a railroad track roaring away to the west.

So I know it will survive. Not even the decline of reading
And the substitution of advertising for genuine pornography
Can crush the uprush of the mushrooming verb
Or drown the overtone of the noun on its own.

Caring

Caring is loving, motionless,
An interval of more and less
Between the stress and the distress.

After the present falls the past,
After the festival, the fast.
Always the deepest is the last.

This is the circle we must trace,
Not spiralled outward, but a space
Returning to its starting place.

Centre of all we mourn and bless,
Centre of calm beyond excess,
Who cares for caring, has caress.

Finis the Cenci

Beatrice, on the high wooden throne,
Surveys the crowded square, the priests, the cross
Before her eyes. She kisses Christ's five wounds.

Beside her, as a sign, her mother's head
Bleeds in the dust. Her brother waits his turn.

She does not let
Those hands approach, but lays aside
Her veil and bodice in so swift a throw
That not a girlish breast is seen
By all the staring multitude
Before she floods her mother.

This is her public modesty, who knew
A father's rape
A father's eye
The driven nail
Her father's blood.

Later they slowly broke her brother's bones.

The Canadian Social Register

*(A Social Register for Canada was promoted in Montreal in 1947.
On the Advisory Committee were names like the Rt Hon. Louis
St Laurent, Sir Ellsworth Flavelle, Air Marshal Bishop, Rear Admiral
Brodeur, the Hon. J. Earl Lawson, Hartland Molson, and others.
A Secret Committee was to screen all applicants. All quotations in
this poem are taken verbatim from the invitation sent out to
prospective members.)*

Reader, we have the honour to invite you to become a "Member of
        the Social Register",
For the paltry fee of $125 per annum.
This "work of art, done in good taste", and listing annually the
        "Notables of the Dominion",
Will contain nothing but "Ladies and Gentlemen pre-eminent in
        the Higher Spheres",
A list, indeed, of "First Families",
Who are "the very fabric of our country".
Thus shall we "build up in the Nation's First Families
A consciousness of their rôle in the life of a civilized democracy".
Thus shall we bring "added dignity and profound significance
To our cultural way of life".
Through deplorable lack of vision, in times past,
Men who were "great Canadians, have everlastingly passed into
        oblivion",
Leaving no "footprints on the sands of time".
Somehow, despite their pre-eminence, they have disappeared.
Shall we, through "tragic shortsightedness", let the leaders of this era
"Disappear into the realm of eternal silence?"
"Shall there be no names, no achievements, to hearten and strengthen
        on-coming generations in time of stress?"
If they have failed to make history, shall they fail to make The
        Canadian Social Register?
No – not if they can pay $125 annually,
And pass our Secret Committee.
For there is a "Secret Committee of seven members",
Who will "determine the eligibility of those applying for
        membership".
Thus will the Social Register be "accepted in the most fastidious
        circles".
And to aid the Secret Committee you will send
The name of your father and the maiden name of your mother,
And the address of your "summer residence"
(For of course you have a summer residence).
You may also submit, with a glossy print of yourself,

"Short quotations from laudatory comments received on diverse
        public occasions".
When printed, the Register will be sent,
Free, gratis, and not even asked for,
To (among many others) the "King of Sweden", the "President of
        Guatemala", and the "Turkish Public Library".

Reader, this will be a "perennial reminder"
Of the people (or such of them as pass the Secret Committee)
Who "fashioned this Canada of ours",
For "One does not live only for toil and gain",
Not, anyway, in First Families. It is comforting to believe
That while we "walk the earth", and pay $125,
And "after we have passed on", there will remain
"In the literature of the Universe", and particularly in the "Turkish
        Public Library",
This "de luxe edition", "these unique and dignified annals",
"These priceless and undying memories", with laudatory comments
        chosen by ourselves,
To which "succeeding First Families and historians alike will look"
For "knowledge, guidance and inspiration".
Lives rich in eligibility will be "written large"
(But within "a maximum of one thousand words")
"For all men to see and judge".
The "glorious dead", too,
These "selfless and noble defenders of Canada's honour",
Will be incorporated in the Social Register
"Without any financial remuneration",
Assuming, of course, that they are all
"Sons and daughters of its Members".

Reader, as you may guess, the Register
Was not "a spur of the moment idea".
It was "long and carefully nurtured".
And "counsel was sought in high and authoritative places",
So that it may "lay a basis upon which prominent Canadians will
        henceforth be appraised
As they go striding down the years",
Paying their $125,
And receiving a "world-wide, gratuitous distribution",
Even unto "the Turkish Public Library".

"Si monumentum requiris, circumspice!"
On this note, we both end.

Eden

Adam stood by a sleeping lion
Feeling its fur with his toes.
He did not hear Eve approaching,
Like a shy fawn she crept close.

The stillness deepened. He turned.
She stood there, too solemn for speech.
He knew that something had happened
Or she never would stay out of reach.

"What is it? What have you found?"
He stared as she held out her hand.
The innocent fruit was shining.
The truth burned like a brand.

"It is good to eat," she said,
"And pleasant to the eyes,
 And—this is the reason I took it—
It is going to make us wise!"

She was like that, the beauty,
Always simple and strong.
She was leading him into trouble
But he could not say she was wrong.

Anyway, what could he do?
She'd already eaten it first.
She could not have all the wisdom.
He'd have to eat and be cursed.

So he ate, and their eyes were opened.
In a flash they knew they were nude.
Their ignorant innocence vanished.
Taste began shaping the crude.

This was no Fall, but Creation,
For although the Terrible Voice
Condemned them to sweat and to labour,
They had conquered the power of choice.

Even God was astonished.
"This man is become one of Us.
If he eat of the Tree of Life . . . !"
Out they went in a rush.

As the Flaming Sword receded
  Eve walked a little ahead.
"If we keep on using this knowledge
  I think we'll be back," she said.

W.L.M.K.

How shall we speak of Canada,
Mackenzie King dead?
The Mother's boy in the lonely room
With his dog, his medium and his ruins?

He blunted us.

We had no shape
Because he never took sides,
And no sides
Because he never allowed them to take shape.

He skilfully avoided what was wrong
Without saying what was right,
And never let his on the one hand
Know what his on the other hand was doing.

The height of his ambition
Was to pile a Parliamentary Committee on a Royal Commission,
To have "conscription if necessary
But not necessarily conscription",
To let Parliament decide –
Later.

Postpone, postpone, abstain.

Only one thread was certain:
After World War I
Business as usual,
After World War II
Orderly decontrol.
Always he led us back to where we were before.

He seemed to be in the centre
Because we had no centre,
No vision
To pierce the smoke-screen of his politics.

Truly he will be remembered
Wherever men honour ingenuity,
Ambiguity, inactivity, and political longevity.

Let us raise up a temple
To the cult of mediocrity,
Do nothing by halves
Which can be done by quarters.

Bonne Entente

The advantages of living with two cultures
Strike one at every turn,
Especially when one finds a notice in an office building:
"This elevator will not run on Ascension Day";
Or reads in the *Montreal Star*:
"Tomorrow being the Feast of the Immaculate Conception,
There will be no collection of garbage in the city";
Or sees on the restaurant menu the bilingual dish:

DEEP APPLE PIE

TARTE AUX POMMES PROFONDES

All the Spikes But the Last

Where are the coolies in your poem, Ned?
Where are the thousands from China who swung their picks with
bare hands at forty below?

Between the first and the million other spikes they drove, and the
dressed-up act of Donald Smith, who has sung their story?

Did they fare so well in the land they helped to unite? Did they get
one of the 25,000,000 CPR acres?
Is all Canada has to say to them written in the Chinese Immigration
Act?

The Bartail Cock

Rounding a look
Her lightened tips
Tackled my fincy
So I gave her the um con.
She was right, all tight,
But clan, did she have mass!

Hatting her pair
She rossed off her tum
Barred at the leer-tender
Tumbled her way to my fable
And cholding my hair
Lissed me on the kips.

I skoated in the fly!

Eclipse

I looked the sun straight in the eye.
He put on dark glasses.

Vision

Vision in long filaments flows
Through the needles of my eyes.
I am fastened to the rose
When it takes me by surprise.

I am clothed in what eye sees.
Snail's small motion, mountain's height,
Dress me with their symmetries
In the robing-rooms of sight.

Summer's silk and winter's wool
Change my inner uniform.
Leaves and grass are cavern cool
As the felted snow is warm.

When the clear and sun-drenched day
Makes a mockery of dress
All the fabric falls away.
I am clothed in nakedness.

Stars so distant, stones nearby
Wait, indifferently, in space
Till an all-perceptive eye
Gives to each its form and place.

Mind is a chameleon
Blending with environment;
To the colours it looks on
Is its own appearance bent.

Yet it changes what it holds
In the knowledge of its gaze
And the universe unfolds
As it multiplies its rays.

Tireless eye, so taut and long,
Touching flowers and flames with ease,
All your wires vibrate with song
When it is the heart that sees.

Flying to Fort Smith

The spread of silver wing
        Gathers us into long lanes of space.
We peer through panes of glass.

The plain of lakes below
        Is bound with bands of green
Fringed by darker green
        Pocked with drops of ponds.

Everywhere
        A huge nowhere,
Underlined by a shy railway.

Snaking brown streams
    At every islanded corner
Widen their reaches
    Leaving blue pools behind.

An arena
    Large as Europe
Silent
    Waiting the contest.

Underground
    In the coins of rock
Cities sleep like seeds.

Mackenzie River

This river belongs
    wholly to itself
        obeying its own laws

Its wide brown eye
    softens what it reflects
        from sky and shore

The top water   calm
    moves purposefully
        to a cold sea

Underneath   its stone bed
    shows sunken rock
        in swirl and surface wave

Suspended
    in its liquid force
        is the soil of deltas

The servient valleys
    reach up to lake and spring
        in clefts of far hills

And shed
    arteries of streams
        that stain the central flood

In spring thaw and spate
    its wide levels
        rise slowly   fall

Like tides
    that start upstream
        and die at sea

A river so Canadian
    it turns its back
        on America

The Arctic shore
    receives the vast flow
        a maze of ponds and dikes

In land so bleak and bare
    a single plume of smoke
        is a scroll of history.

Mount Royal

No things sit, set, hold. All swim,
Whether through space of cycle, rock or sea.
This mountain of Mount Royal marks the hours
On earth's sprung clock. Look how where
This once was island, lapped by salty waves,
And now seems fixed with sloping roads and homes.
Where flowers march, I dig these tiny shells
Once deep-down fishes safe, it seemed, on sand.
What! Sand, mud, silt, where now commuters go
About their civic clatter! Boulevards
Where crept the shiny mollusc! Time is big
With eon seconds now, its pendulum
Swung back to ice-pressed pole-cap, that drove down
This chest of earth, until the melting came
And left a hollow cavity for seas
To make into a water waiting-room.
But sea-bed floated slowly, surely up
As weight released brought in-breath back to earth
And ground uprising drove the water back
In one more tick of clock. Pay taxes now,
Elect your boys, lay out your pleasant parks,
You gill-lunged, quarrelsome ephemera!
The tension tightens yearly, underneath,
A folding continent shifts silently
And oceans wait their turn for ice or streets.

A. J. M.
SMITH

A. J. M. Smith was born in Montreal in 1902 and entered McGill in 1921, where he received a B.SC. in 1925 and an M.A. in 1926. He then attended Edinburgh University from 1926 to 1928 and completed his work for the PH.D. in 1931. As a graduate student his special academic interests seem to have been Yeats and seventeenth-century religious poetry (he published an essay on Vaughan in 1933). At McGill he contributed over forty poems to a magazine which he helped to found, *The McGill Fortnightly Review* (1925-1927). But his poetry also appeared elsewhere during the twenties and thirties, in American magazines like *The Dial* and *The Nation*, in the London *Adelphi* and *New Verse*, and in *The Canadian Forum*. His criticism includes a vigorous essay called "Canadian Poetry – A Minority Report" in the *University of Toronto Quarterly* (January, 1939). But no volume of his poetry appeared before the war, although a dozen poems were included in the important Canadian anthology *New Provinces* (Macmillan, 1936). It was in 1943 that Smith's talents as poet and critic (already well known to a few) achieved a more general recognition with the publication by Ryerson of his *News of the Phoenix* (which won the Governor General's Award for poetry) and the publication by Gage of his discriminating and influential anthology *The Book of Canadian Poetry.* The latter has been reprinted a number of times (and brought up to date in 1958); the first volume of its prose companion has recently been published (Gage, 1965), and its bilingual successor, *The Oxford Book of Canadian Verse,* came out in 1960. Smith has also published two more collections of his own poetry, *A Sort of Ecstasy* (Michigan State College Press, and Ryerson, 1954) and *Collected Poems* (Oxford, 1962). Since 1936 Smith has been a member of the English Department of Michigan State University, although he returns to Canada regularly and has spent the occasional summer or even year teaching at Canadian universities such as Queen's and Dalhousie. Throughout his career Smith's conscious standards of excellence have remained remarkably consistent. Desmond Pacey quotes from a letter which Smith wrote to him in 1957: "Metaphysical poetry and pure poetry are what I stood and stand for."

Like an Old Proud King in a Parable

A bitter king in anger to be gone
From fawning courtier and doting queen
Flung hollow sceptre and gilt crown away,
And breaking bound of all his counties green
He made a meadow in the northern stone
And breathed a palace of inviolable air
To cage a heart that carolled like a swan,
And slept alone, immaculate and gay,
With only his pride for a paramour.

O who is that bitter king? It is not I.

Let me, I beseech thee, Father, die
From this fat royal life, and lie
As naked as a bridegroom by his bride,
And let that girl be the cold goddess Pride:

And I will sing to the barren rock
Your difficult, lonely music, heart,
Like an old proud king in a parable.

Swift Current

This is a visible
and crystal wind:
no ragged edge,
no splash of foam,
no whirlpool's scar;
only
– in the narrows,
sharpness cutting sharpness,
arrows of direction,
spears of speed.

Sea Cliff

Wave on wave
and green on rock
and white between
the splash and black
the crash and hiss
of the feathery fall,
the snap and shock
of the water wall
and the wall of rock:

after –
after the ebb-flow,
wet rock,
high –
high over the slapping green,
water sliding away
and the rock abiding,
new rock riding
out of the spray.

The Lonely Land

Cedar and jagged fir
uplift sharp barbs
against the gray
and cloud-piled sky;
and in the bay
blown spume and windrift
and thin, bitter spray
snap
at the whirling sky;
and the pine trees
lean one way.

A wild duck calls
to her mate,
and the ragged
and passionate tones
stagger and fall,
and recover,
and stagger and fall,
on these stones –
are lost
in the lapping of water
on smooth, flat stones.

This is a beauty
of dissonance,
this resonance
of stony strand,
this smoky cry
curled over a black pine
like a broken
and wind-battered branch
when the wind
bends the tops of the pines
and curdles the sky
from the north.

This is the beauty
of strength
broken by strength
and still strong.

In the Wilderness

He walks alone, uncomforted,
In spring's green ripple, autumn's red.

Birds, like dark starlight,
Twinkle in the sky, are light

As feathers blown about in a gale,
And their song is as cold and sharp as hail.

The lonely air and the hard ground
Are crying to him with no sound

Words that the hurdy-gurdy year
Whines ceaselessly in his sad ear.

He walks between the green leaf and the red
Like one who follows a beloved dead,

And with a young, pedantic eye
Observes how still the dead do lie.

His gaze is stopped in the hard earth,
And cannot penetrate to heaven's mirth.

A Hyacinth for Edith

Now that the ashen rain of gummy April
Clacks like a weedy and stain'd mill,

So that all the tall purple trees
Are pied porpoises in swishing seas,

And the yellow horses and milch cows
Come out of their long frosty house

To gape at the straining flags
The brown pompous hill wags,

I'll seek within the wood's black plinth
A candy-sweet sleek wooden hyacinth –

And in its creaking naked glaze,
And in the varnish of its blaze,

The bird of ecstasy shall sing again,
The bearded sun shall spring again –

A new ripe fruit upon the sky's high tree,
A flowery island in the sky's wide sea –

And childish cold ballades, long dead, long mute,
Shall mingle with the gayety of bird and fruit,

And fall like cool and soothing rain
On all the ardour, all the pain

Lurking within this tinsel paradise
Of trams and cinemas and manufactured ice,

Till I am grown again my own lost ghost
Of joy, long lost, long given up for lost,

And walk again the wild and sweet wildwood
Of our lost innocence, our ghostly childhood.

I Shall Remember

I shall remember forever
A lonely swallow swerving
Over a dusky river,
Sweeping and solemnly curving
In long arcs that never
Stirred the still stream,
For so your smile
Curves in quiet dream
For a slow sleepy while
Over your tranquil mind
That is not stirred
Even by thought's faintest wind,
Or fancy's loneliest bird.

To the Haggard Moon

Damn'd haggard moon
you fix me with your glare

When shall the sun
like a good fairy

drive you
into your grave again

and turn your black palace
to a shining meadow?

To a Young Poet
For C.A.M.

Tread the metallic nave
Of this windless day with
A pace designed and grave:
– Iphigenia in her myth

Creating for stony eyes
An elegant, fatal dance
Was signed with no device
More alien to romance

Than I would have you find
In the stern, autumnal face
Of Artemis, whose kind
Cruelty makes duty grace,

Whose votary alone
Seals the affrighted air
With the worth of a hard thing done
Perfectly, as though without care.

The Plot Against Proteus

This is a theme for muted coronets
To dangle from debilitated heads
Of navigation, kings, or riverbeds
That rot or rise what time the seamew sets
Her course by stars among the smoky tides
Entangled. Old saltencrusted Proteus treads
Once more the watery shore that water weds
While rocking fathom bell rings round and rides.

Now when the blind king of the water thinks
The sharp hail of the salt out of his eyes
To abdicate, run thou, O Prince, and fall
Upon him. This cracked walrus skin that stinks
Of the rank sweat of a mermaid's thighs
Cast off, and nab him; when you have him, call.

Choros

Moveless, unmoved, caught in the dead face,
The torches make a slow wound on the gray mist,
A ragged circle the colour of fox fur.

Sharp beak and still, translucent water kiss:
Wry lips, dank hair, taut throat, and marble eyes
Mix in the pulpy salt of foam, and hiss.

Knifethrust of silver, sunlight on fishscales,
Waves out of the bay's bound, Iô! Now the new wind
Wafts Iphigenia from Aulis, bellies our creaking sails.

The Fountain

This fountain sheds her flowery spray
Like some enchanted tree of May
Immortalized in feathery frost
With nothing but its fragrance lost.

Yet nothing has been done amiss
In this white metamorphosis,
For fragrance here has grown to form,
And Time is fooled, although he storm.

Through Autumn's sodden disarray
These blossoms fall, but not away;
They build a tower of silver light
Where Spring holds court in Winter's night;
And while chaotic darkness broods
The golden groves to solitudes,
Here shines, in this transfigured spray,
The cold, immortal ghost of day.

News of the Phoenix

They say the Phoenix is dying, some say dead.
Dead without issue is what one message said,
But that has been suppressed, officially denied.

I think myself the man who sent it lied.
In any case, I'm told, he has been shot,
As a precautionary measure, whether he did or not.

The Shrouding

Unravel this curdled cloud,
Wash out the stain of the sun,
Let the winding of your shroud
Be delicately begun.

Bind up the muddy Thames,
Hearken the arrogant worm,
Sew the seams and the hems
With fine thread and firm.

When the moon is a sickle of ice
Reaping a sheaf of stars,
Put pennies on your eyes,
Lie you down long and sparse.

Fold your thin hands like this,
Over your breast, so;
Protract no farewell kiss,
No ceremonial woe,

But stand up in your shroud
Above the crumbling bone,
Drawn up like one more cloud
Into the radiant sun.

Prothalamium

Here in this narrow room there is no light;
The dead tree sings against the window pane;
Sand shifts a little, easily; the wall
Responds a little, inchmeal, slowly, down.

My sister, whom my dust shall marry, sleeps
Alone, yet knows what bitter root it is
That stirs within her; see, it splits the heart —
Warm hands grown cold, grown nerveless as a fin,
And lips enamelled to a hardness —
Consummation ushered in
By wind in sundry corners.

This holy sacrament was solemnized
In harsh poetics a good while ago —
At Malfy and the Danish battlements,
And by that preacher from a cloud in Paul's.

No matter: each must read the truth himself,
Or, reading it, reads nothing to the point.
Now these are me, whose thought is mine, and hers,
Who are alone here in this narrow room —
Tree fumbling pane, bell tolling,
Ceiling dripping and the plaster falling,
And Death, the voluptuous, calling.

The Archer

Bend back thy bow, O Archer, till the string
Is level with thine ear, thy body taut,
Its nature art, thyself thy statue wrought
Of marble blood, thy weapon the poised wing
Of coiled and aquiline Fate. Then, loosening, fling
The hissing arrow like a burning thought
Into the empty sky that smokes as the hot
Shaft plunges to the bullseye's quenching ring.

So for a moment, motionless, serene,
Fixed between time and time, I aim and wait;
Nothing remains for breath now but to waive
His prior claim and let the barb fly clean
Into the heart of what I know and hate –
That central black, the ringed and targeted grave.

Field of Long Grass

When she walks in the field of long grass
The delicate little hands of the grass
Lean forward a little to touch her.

Light is like the waving of the long grass.
Light is the faint to and fro of her dress.
Light rests for a while in her bosom.

When it is all gone from her bosom's hollow
And out of the field of long grass,
She walks in the dark by the edge of the fallow land.

Then she begins to walk in my heart.
Then she walks in me, swaying in my veins.

My wrists are a field of long grass
A little wind is kissing.

No Treasure

Sew up the ragged lips
Where the red worm bleeds;
Time's candle drips,
And the light secedes
From this man and his needs.

Pile no memorial mound,
Smooth the raw fissure:
Why should this place be found?
To whom could that give pleasure?
This is no buried treasure.

The Circle

Over me the summer drips,
And over me the wind cries;
The tree above me sways and dips,
The bird above me sings, and flies.

Insensibly the season slips
From coloured days to paler days,
With faded berries on my lips,
And in my eyes an autumn haze

That thickens to a wintry mist
Of amethyst and drifting snow,
Of drifting snow and amethyst
That dances solemnly and slow.

My breath goes ghostly on the air;
I move my lips, but cannot call,
Nor break the quietude I share
With earth and sky, with brook and fall.

Silent, enraptured, I remain;
The many-coloured seasons pass:
Now April sunshine, April rain,
Lights crocuses among the grass;

And now the oozing summer drips
Through heavy days of slow delight:
The tree above me sways and dips,
The bird above is poised for flight.

The Mermaid

Dark green and seaweed-cold, the snake-bright hair
Streams on the golden-sun-illumined wave
That sways as gently as two bells the grave
Small coral-tinted breasts to starboard there
Where salt translucency's green branches bear
This sea-rose, a lost mermaid, whose cold cave,
Left lightless now, the lapping seatides lave
At base of Okeanos' twisted stair.

She's come where bubbles burst, crisp silver skims;
Where the tall sun stands naked; where he shines;
Where live men walk the shrouds with fork-like limbs.

She smiles: and the head of the shipmite swims;
But the bo'sun bawls for the grappling lines,
And the Chaplain fumbles in his book of hymns.

The Sorcerer

There is a sorcerer in Lachine
Who for a small fee will put a spell
On my beloved, who has sea-green
Eyes, and on my doting self as well.

He will transform us, if we like, to goldfish:
We shall swim in a crystal bowl,
And the bright water will go swish
Over our naked bodies; we shall have no soul.

In the morning the syrupy sunshine
Will dance on our tails and fins.
I shall have her then all for mine,
And Father Lebeau will hear no more of her sins.

Come along, good sir, change us into goldfish.
I would put away intellect and lust,
Be but a red gleam in a crystal dish,
But kin of the trembling ocean, not of the dust.

Chinoiserie

After Théophile Gautier

It is not you, no, madam, whom I love,
Nor you either, Juliet, nor you,
Ophelia, nor Beatrice, nor that dove,
Fair-haired Laura with the big eyes; No.

She is in China whom I love just now;
She lives at home and cares for her old parents;
From a tower of porcelain she leans her brow,
By the Yellow River, where haunt the cormorants.

She has upward-slanting eyes, a foot to hold
In your hand – that small; the colour shed
By lamps is less clear than her coppery gold;
And her long nails are stained with carmine red.

From her trellis she leans out so far
That the dipping swallows are within her reach,
And like a poet, to the evening star
She sings the willow and the flowering peach.

Brigadier

A Song of French Canada

One Sunday morning soft and fine
Two old campaigners let their nags meander;
One was a Sergeant of the Line,
The other a Brigade Commander.
The General spoke with martial roar,
"Nice weather for this time of year!"
    And *"Right you are,"* replied Pandore,
    "Right you are, my Brigadier."

"A Guardsman's is a thankless calling,
 Protecting private property,
In summer or when snows are falling,
 From malice, rape, or robbery;
While the wife whom I adore
Sleeps alone and knows no cheer."
    And *"Right you are,"* replied Pandore,
    "Right you are, my Brigadier."

"I have gathered Glory's laurel
 With the rose of Venus twined –
I am Married, and a General;
 Yet, by Jesus, I've a mind
To start like Jason for the golden shore
And follow my Star – away from here!"
    "Ah, right you are," replied Pandore,
    "Right you are, my Brigadier."

"I remember the good days of my youth
 And the old songs that rang
So cheerily. In that time, forsooth,
 I had a doting mistress, full of tang . . .
But, ah! the heart – I know not wherefore –
Loves to change its bill of fare."
    And *"Right you are,"* replied Pandore,
    "Right you are, my Brigadier."

Now Phoebus neared his journey's end;
Our heroes' shadows fell behind:
Yet still the Sergeant did attend,
And still the General spoke his mind.
"Observe," he said, "how more and more
Yon orb ensanguines all the sphere."
    And *"Right you are," replied Pandore,*
    "Right you are, my Brigadier."

They rode in silence for a while:
You only heard the measured tread
Of muffled hoof beats, mile on mile –
But when Aurora, rosy red,
Unbarred her Eastern door,
The faint refrain still charmed the ear,
    As "Right you are," replied Pandore,
    "Right you are, my Brigadier."

Quietly to be Quickly or Other or Ether

A Song or a Dance

To be
to be quietly
to be quietly to be
to be quick
Not this but that

To be
to be either
to be either
or other
Is this a bother?
Take ether

Some see
Some see
this is not that
This is what

some see
Some see this
Some see what
not all see

Quietly to be quick
not this but that
other or ether
Do you see?

What the Emanation
of Casey Jones
Said to the Medium

Turn inward on the brain
The flashlight of an I,
While the express train
Time, unflagged, roars by.

Pick out the dirt of stars,
Wipe off the wires of gut,
Uncouple the foetid cars
From the spangled banner of smut.

Then shine, O curdled orb,
Within thy vantage box,
Field that attracts, absorbs
Cats, hairpins, spring greens, clocks,

That twists like vapor, seeps
From tunnel's murky bung
Hole, fogs the vista-dome and creeps
Away, accomplished and undone.

Take note of freedom's prize,
Dissolve and walk the wind,
Ride camels through the eyes
Of moles – the make-up of the mind

Embellishes and protects,
Draws beards between fabulous tits,
Endorses the stranger's checks,
Judges and always acquits.

Turn inward to the brain:
The signal stars are green,
Unheard the ghost train
Time, and Death can not be seen.

To Henry Vaughan

Homesick? and yet your country Walks
Were heaven'd for you. Such bright stalks
Of grasses! such pure Green! such blue
Clear skies! such light! such silver dew! –
On each brief bud and shining twig
White pregnant jewels, each one big
With meaning, rich pearls cast before
Not swine but men, who toss or snore.
   Thou didst not so: thou wert awake;
And stirring forth before the break
Of day, thou wouldst enquire
If, with the Cock, no angel choir
Meant to announce th'eternal Day;
If, in the sun's first quick'ning ray
Thou might'st observe the flaming hair
Of thy wish'd Lord, thy Bridegroom dear.
   Yet when the Constellations fine
Stand where the sun before did shine,
You may not in your good-night pray'r
Ask day more holy, heav'n more near:
Earth's angels, these tall feathery trees,
Sang in thy loved one's praise; thy bees
Gather'd his Honey; one small bird
In three clear notes his Name preferr'd.
   Celestial strings might not surpass
Thy morning breezes in long grass;
The slow rain from the laden tree,
Dropping from heaven, brought to thee

Sounds of the purest harmony,
Setting thy caged soul free to fly,
Borne on the breath of fruits and flow'rs
Sweeten'd and made fresh in silver show'rs.
    And add to these thy bubbling rills;
Soft winds; the intricate rich trills
Of happy larks that climb the air
Like a broad golden winding Stair
To Heaven, singing as they climb,
Lifting the rapt soul out of Time
Into a long Eternity
Where Heaven is now, and still to be.
    Yet art thou Homesick! to be gone
From all this brave Distraction
Wouldst seal thine ear, nail down thine eye;
To be one perfect Member, die;
And anxious to exchange in death
Thy foul, for thy Lord's precious, breath,
Thou art content to beg a pall,
Glad to be Nothing, to be All.

Astræa Redux
KEEWAYDIN POETRY CONFERENCE

For Kim and Doug Jones

Coming over the water
paddling an old boat
with a broken board
and a bottle in a paper bag

Leaning into the wind
making out an old wharf
in a new land
and a doubtful call

A boy or a female figure
seen in the distance

Nearer, a coughing motor
then a spate of spaniels
leaping and frisking
with Stuart curls
and long sad faces

Coming to land
coming home

to the good people
known anew

My people   lordly ones
the Duke of Dudek   His Grace of Layton
and with me Scott
diaconal, archbishopric
twisted benevolent
with needle eye

Known anew,   loved always
... always ... now ...
Royalists   Yr. most obt. servant

Memo: *Not to go on my travels again*

Thomas Moore and Sweet Annie

My honey, my cunny, my cosy, my dear,
Hold me and hug me and call me your bear;
Tip me and tup me and bed me down tight,
And we'll raise a commotion of love and delight.

Embrace me, enlace me, and roll me around;
I'll dance o'er the waves, and I'll plant a new ground:
I'll settle, establish, be king o' the isle,
And find my reward in my sweet Annie's smile.

The Wisdom of Old Jelly Roll

How all men wrongly death to dignify
Conspire, I tell. Parson, poetaster, pimp,
Each acts or acquiesces. They prettify,
Dress up, deodorize, embellish, primp,
And make a show of Nothing. Ah, but met-
aphysics laughs: she touches, tastes, and smells
– Hence knows – the diamond holes that make a net.
Silence resettled testifies to bells.
"Nothing" depends on "Thing", which is or was:
So death makes life or makes life's worth, a worth
Beyond all highfalutin' woes or shows
To publish and confess. "Cry at the birth,
Rejoice at the death," old Jelly Roll said,
Being on whisky, ragtime, chicken, and the scriptures fed.

A Narrow Squeak

Variations on a Theme
of Anne Wilkinson

I shut my eyes and turned round thrice
And opened them again: the day was gone;
A bloodshot moonlight crept along,
And the green hills were caked with ice.

Who was it wavered in the frosty air,
Looked back and hesitated, turned away,
But waited – with a word to say?
She moved her lips. I could not hear,

I could not hear the word she said.
It was a word of life or death.
It stoned my heart, it stopped my breath.
I dropped like stone, I dropped down dead.

The ground swung round three times I think.
I pushed my heavy lids apart;
I drank the air; I felt my heart;
It moved, and I could smile or wink.

My eyelids fluttered: all returned –
Bright day, green grass, soft air, warm love –
No bloodshot moon at all, but high above,
Just as before, the gold sun burned.

On Knowing Nothing

Others have seen men die
Or heard a woman scream
One last word *Never!*
How do I know the horror
That breaks the dream,
Hateful yet clung to
As the image hugs the mirror
With such a silver shiver
As chills and almost kills?

I know: but how or why
Out of this savory fatness I
Should suck the sharp surmise
That strangles dying eyes
I do not know. What have I done
To bring the Angel round my head
That I can smell his pinion
(Bond or wing?)
Whom I must hate and love?

The surgeon's jab, a woman's thigh
Give blank surcease
For short or long.
I cannot let the hollow
Interval alone,
But pick it like a scab
To probe the wound within –
As deep, as nothing, as the grave.

DOROTHY
LIVESAY

Born in Winnipeg in 1909 (both parents were writers), Dorothy
Livesay moved to Toronto in 1920, and in 1927 she enrolled at Trinity
College in the University of Toronto. Her course was Moderns
(French and Italian), but already in her second year she had managed
to publish a small collection of poetry called *Green Pitcher* (Mac-
millan, 1928). One of her undergraduate years was spent in France
at the University of Aix-Marseilles and after graduation from
Toronto in 1931, she did graduate work at the Sorbonne on the
relations between the French symbolists and their English successors.
But when she returned in 1933 to the Canada of the depression, she
briefly attended the School of Social Work in Toronto and then
pursued her newly chosen career as a social worker in a number of
places in Canada and the United States. She ended up in Vancouver,
where, after marrying in 1937, she continued to live and raise a
family. She was sent by UNESCO to teach English in Northern
Rhodesia at a Teacher Training College from 1960 to 1963, and on
her return to Vancouver she did graduate work and teaching with
the Department of English and the newly formed Department of

Writing at the University of British Columbia. She spent 1966-1967 as Writer-in-Residence at the University of New Brunswick. She is a member of the Unitarian Church.

Dorothy Livesay's second book, *Signposts* (Macmillan, 1932), continued the imagistic and somewhat epigrammatic quality of her first, but in the thirties she added to this a new expansiveness of form and style and a new range of social and industrial material. The latter is particularly obvious in *Day and Night* (Ryerson, 1944), which was followed by *Poems for People* (Ryerson, 1947). *Call My People Home* (Ryerson, 1949), *New Poems* (Emblem Books, 1955) and *The Colour of God's Face* (privately printed, 1964) are small pamphlets, but the *Selected Poems* (Ryerson, 1957) is a representative selection from her whole output to that year. She is the sort of poet who never loses her earlier qualities, but is continually adding to them what she learns from new experiences and new writers. Her latest work will be appearing in *The Unquiet Bed* (Ryerson, 1967).

Fire and Reason

I cannot shut out the night –
Nor its sharp clarity.

The many blinds we draw,
You and I,
The many fires we light
Can never quite obliterate
The irony of stars.
The deliberate moon,
The last unsolved finality
Of night.

A Boy in Bronze

Too grave for ecstasy:
Merely intent
On stringing your fine bow.
Just so,
Arrows in readiness,
As if to say
(If you could find the words)
"This matters very much to me:
I must aim straight."
Unconscious of your body's symmetry
Its young desire
Its growing urge
For flight.

In the Street

In rainy weather
Who can tell
Whether we weep
Or not?

I dread the sun
For his fierce honesty.

Wilderness Stone

I dreamed that I dwelt in a house
On the edge of a field
With a fire for warmth
And a roof for shield.

But when I awoke I saw
There was nothing at all
But rain for my roof
And wind for my wall.

Going to Sleep

I shall lie like this when I am dead –
But with one more secret in my head.

Green Rain

I remember long veils of green rain
Feathered like the shawl of my grandmother –
Green from the half-green of the spring trees
Waving in the valley.

I remember the road
Like the one which leads to my grandmother's house,
A warm house, with green carpets,
Geraniums, a trilling canary
And shining horse-hair chairs;
And the silence, full of the rain's falling
Was like my grandmother's parlour
Alive with herself and her voice, rising and falling –
Rain and wind intermingled.

I remember on that day
I was thinking only of my love
And of my love's house.
But now I remember the day
As I remember my grandmother.
I remember the rain as the feathery fringe of her shawl.

Farewell

A stranger walks now in my shoes.
– So, House, goodbye! she calls.
But I remain, to run unheard
Barefooted through the halls.

A stranger shuts the gate. But I
Stand grieving close to you:
We pluck a leaf, or toss a stone –
Not knowing what to do.

Night falls: so we must turn within,
My footsteps echoes, where
Your heavy boots go stamping up
The old familiar stair.

A mirror at the top: there you
Regard your own sad face
And think me gone – although I stand
Fast rooted to this place.

Sun

This sunlight spills the answer, and is swift
To magnetize my passion, draw it forth
For you or any man to look upon.
I am as earth upturned, alive with seed
For summer's silence and for autumn's fire.
I am as bound as earth, yet wholly free
As the slow early wind that trails the breath
Of hidden wood-anemones.
I am all things I would not let you know
Save that, in knowing spring, they are displayed:
The softest singing from a thrush's throat
Tells you my thought before I breathe a word.
I may escape – you hold my body still
In stretching out your hand to feel the wind.

From the Husk

From the husk of the old world
To the new I fly
Strong wings beating
In a bluer sky

Where old men stretch not
Their vampire necks
And young men vaunt not
Their sunburnt backs

Where jewelled women
With glittering breasts
Suck not the life-blood
From young nests

But where the cradled
Infant rocks
While cloudy sheep
Caress his locks.

And where the golden
Apples blow
In easy bliss
Upon a bough.

Day and Night

I

Dawn, red and angry, whistles loud and sends
A geysered shaft of steam searching the air.
Scream after scream announces that the churn
Of life must move, the giant arm command.
Men in a stream, a human moving belt
Move into sockets, every one a bolt.
The fun begins, a humming whirring drum –
Men do a dance in time to the machines.

One step forward
Two steps back
Shove the lever,
Push it back

While Arnot whirls
A roundabout
And Geoghan shuffles
Bolts about

One step forward
Hear it crack
Smashing rhythm—
Two steps back.

Your heart-beat pounds
Against your throat
The roaring voices
Drown your shout

Across the way
A writhing whack
Sets you spinning
Two steps back—

One step forward
Two steps back.

II

Day and night rising and falling
Night and day shift gears and slip rattling
Down the runway, shot into storerooms
Where only eyes and a notebook remember
The record of evil, the sum of commitments.
We move as through sleep's revolving memories
Piling up hatred, stealing the remnants
Doors forever folding before us—
And where is the recompense, on what agenda
Will you set love down? Who knows of peace?

Day and night
Night and day
Light rips into ribbons
What we say

I called to love
Deep in dream:
Be with me in the daylight
As in gloom.

Be with me in the pounding
In the knives against my back
Set your voice resounding
Above the steel's whip crack.

High and sweet
Sweet and high
Hold, hold up the sunlight
In the sky!

Day and night
Night and day
Tear up all the silence
Find the words I could not say . . .

III

We were stoking coal in the furnaces; red hot
They gleamed, burning our skins away, his and mine.
We were working together, night and day, and knew
Each other's stroke; and without words exchanged
An understanding about kids at home,
The landlord's jaw, wage-cuts and overtime.

We were like buddies, see? Until they said
That nigger is too smart the way he smiles
And sauces back the foreman; he might say
Too much one day, to others changing shifts.
Therefore they cut him down, who flowered at night
And raised me up, day hanging over night—
So furnaces could still consume our withered skin.

Shadrack, Mechak and Abednego
Turn in the furnace, whirling slow.

> Lord, I'm burnin' in the fire
> Lord, I'm steppin' on the coal
> Lord, I'm blacker than my brother
> Blow your breath down here.

> Boss, I'm smothered in the darkness
> Boss, I'm shrivellin' in the flames
> Boss, I'm blacker than my brother
> Blow your breath down here.

Shadrack, Mechak and Abednego
Burn in the furnace, whirling slow.

IV

Up in the roller room, men swing steel
Swing it, zoom; and cut it, crash.
Up in the dark the welder's torch
Makes sparks fly like lightning's reel.

Now I remember storm on a field:
The trees bow tense before the blow
Even the jittering sparrow's talk
Ripples into the still tree shield.

We are in storm that has no cease
No lull before, no after time
When green with rain the grasses grow
And air is sweet with fresh increase.

We bear the burden home to bed
The furnace glows within our hearts:
Our bodies hammered through the night
Are welded into bitter bread.

Bitter, yes:
But listen, friend,
We are mightier
In the end

We have ears
Alert to seize
A weakness in
The foreman's ease.

We have eyes
To look across
The bosses' profit
At our loss.

Are you waiting?
Wait with us
Every evening
There's a hush

Use it not
For love's slow count:
Add up hate
And let it mount –

One step forward
Two steps back
Will soon be over:
Hear it crack!

The wheels may whirr
A roundabout
And neighbour's shuffle
Drown your shout

The wheel must limp
Till it hangs still
And crumpled men
Pour down the hill:

Day and night
Night and day –
Till life is turned
The other way!

Prelude for Spring

These dreams abound:
Foot's leap to shore
Above the sound
Of river's roar –
Disabled door
Banged and barricaded
Then on, on
Furrow, fawn
Through wall and wood
So fast no daring could
Tear off the hood
Unmask the soul pursued.

Slash underbrush
Tear bough and branch
Seek cover, rabbit's burrow –
Hush!

He comes. Insistent, sure
Proud prowler, this pursuer comes
Noiseless, no wind-stir
No leaf-turn over;
Together quiet creeps on twig,
Hush hovers in his hands.

How loud heart's thump –
Persistent pump
Sucks down, down sap
Then up in surge
(Axe striking stump).

How breezy breath –
Too strong a wind
Scatters a stir
Where feathers are,
Bustles a bough.

How blind two eyes
Shuttling to-fro
Not weaving light
Nor sight . . .
In darkness flow.

(Only the self is loud;
World's whisperless.)

Dive down then, scuttle under;
Run, fearless of feet's thunder.
Somehow, the road rolls back in mist
Here is the meadow where we kissed
And here the horses, galloping
We rode upon in spring . . .

O beat of air, wing beat
Scatter of rain, sleet,
Resisting leaves,
Retarding feet

And drip of rain, leaf drip
Sting on cheek and lip
Tearing pores
With lash of whip

And hoof's away, heart's hoof
Down greening lanes, with roof
Of cherry blow
And apple puff –

O green wet, sun lit
Soaked earth's glitter!
Down mouth, to munch
Up hoof, to canter

Through willow lanes
A gold-shaft shower,
Embracing elms
That lack leaf-lustre

And copse' cool bed
All lavendered
With scentless, sweet
Hepatica –

Till side by side
In fields' brown furrow
Swathe sunlight over
Every shadow!

But still
On heart's high hill
And summit of
A day's delight
Still will he stoop to brush
From heaven's height
Soaring unspent,
Still will he stoop to brush
Wing tip on hair,
Fan mind with fear.

And now the chill
Raw sun
Goes greener still –
The sky
Cracks like an icicle:

Frozen, foot-locked
Heart choked and chafed
Wing-battered and unsafe,
Grovel to ground!
A cry
Lashes the sky –

These dreams abound.

Annunciation

I

Your face is new; strange;
Yet infinitely known
Loved in some century
Grass swept, tree sown.

I memorize
The lineaments, so lean:
Steel bird prey intent
Flight imminent

I see your stride (no walk)
Cleaving the air,
Cloud treading, your hair
Sickle bent.

O early, early
Before dawn whispers
Before day fingers
The faulty doorway

Early in the late
Moon-tossed night
Your face a flash
Foreruns the light.

Fantasia

And I have learned how diving's done
How breathing air, cool wafted trees
Clouds massed above the man-made tower
How these
Can live no more in eye and ear:
And mind be dumb
To all save Undine and her comb.

Imagination's underworld! where child goes down
Light as a feather. Water pressure
Hardly holds him, diving's easy
As the flight of bird in air
Or bomber drumming to his lair.

Child goes down, and laughingly
(He's not wanted yet, you see)
Catches fishes in his hand
Burrows toe in shifting sand
Seizes all the weeds about
To make a small sub-rosa boat

Then up he bobs, as easily
As any blown balloon
To greet the bosky, brooding sky
And hunger for the sun.

.　.　.　.

And child grown taller, clothed in man's
Long limbs, and shaggy hair, his chin outthrust
Searches for years the rounded world
Climbs to its peaks, falls to its valleys green
Striding the trim and trailing towns
Fingering the fond arteries
Possessing things, and casting them
Cloakwise to earth for sleeping time . . .

Sometime the lust wanderer
Will sleep, will pause; will dream of plunging deep
Below it all, where he will need
No clock companion, thorn in flesh, no contact man
To urge him from the ground.
For flying's easy, if you do it diving
And diving is the self unmoored
Ranging and roving – man alone.

.　.　.　.

And I have learned how diving's done
Wherefore the many, many
Chose the watery stair
Down, down Virginia
With your feted hair
Following after Shelley
Or wordcarvers I knew –
Here is the fascination
Of the salty stare:
And death is here.
Death courteous and calm, glass-smooth
His argument so suave, so water-worn
A weighted stone.

And death's deliberation, his
Most certain waiting-room
His patience with the patient, who will be
His for infinity . . .

So no astounded peerers
On the surface craft
No dragging nets, no cranes
No gnarled and toughened rope
Not any prayer nor pulley man-devised
Will shake the undersea
Or be
More than a brief torpedo, children's arrow
More than a gaudy top outspun
Its schedule done . . .

   .   .   .   .

Wise to have learned: how diving's done
How breathing air, cool wafted trees
Clouds massed above the man-made tower
How these
Can live no more in eye and ear:
And mind be dumb
To all save Undine and her comb . . .

Abracadabra

On a wicked afternoon
When the witch is there
When night's downsnare
Swoops like a loon
Strafing the air
On a wicked afternoon

In the witty time of day
When the mind's at play
The cat's at call
The guitar off the wall
Wind holds sway
In the witty time of day

Then the witch will walk
Full of witty talk
And the cat will stalk
Tail high as a cock

The guitar in the room
Will fuss and fume
Strumming at the tune
For a wicked afternoon

And out in the park
Wind will unfrock
The autumn trees
And falling leaves
Shiver with shock –

And Time with his
Weaving, wailing horn
Shivers my timbers
Shatters my corn:

(Little boy blue
Blows a blue tune
On a wicked afternoon.)

Of Mourners

Mourn not for man, speeding to lay waste
The essence of a countryside's most chaste
And ageless contour; her cool-breasted hills,
Purled streams, bare choirs in wood, fair daffodils –

Mourn not, as maudlin singers did, the scars
Left by the slag, industrial wars,
Men tearing fields apart for railway towns
Wresting the silly sheep from sleepy downs:

And sing no more the sentimental song
Of spinning jenny holding lads too long,
Of children toiling underground, or laws
For hanging witches, burning corn for cause.

Sing only with the gibing Chaucer's tongue
Of foible and grave fault; of words unsung,
More pungent victory than battles won:
Sing deeds neglected, desecrations done

Not on the lovely body of the world
But on man's building heart, his shaping soul.
Mourn, with me, the intolerant, hater of sun:
Child's mind maimed before he learns to run.

Improvisations on an Old Theme

If I must go, let it be easy, slow
The curve complete, and a sure swerve
To the goal. Let it be slow and sweet
To know how leaf consumes its time,
How petal sucks to the sun's heat;
Or as old bones, settling into sail,
Eyes too remote for earth's light
Set on a solar circle, whose bright
Business brims the universe.

Let me know well how the winds blow
Smoky in Autumn with leaf reek;
And summer's sleek surrender
Touching the maple; let my branches sigh
For snow, and in a muffled mantle, let me go.

Keep me for quiet. Save me ever from
Disastrous ending sounding without drum,
No decent exhalation of the breath –
The dazzling violence of atomic death.

London Revisited (1946)

I

In the cavern of cold
Chill of the world
Turn of the old
Year's leaf to the soil
September to sere
In the cave of the year

The long fingered wall
Of the house disembowelled
Stares in a prayer
Voiceless, unvowelled:
Inerasably stained
The stone is unveiled.

(But down in the pit
Where the cellar was hit
It is green, it is gold:
From the grass and leaf mould
Willow herb's knit
With goldenrod's hold).

In the cave of the year
The underground ride
Heart knocks in fear
Map is no guide –
Whose is this hand
Chained to your side?

II

Once it was death's. We saw
The bone of the beast
Stretcher bearer's torch
Flashed on his dark feast

Once in the tense sky
Rivetted with blood
We visioned blank defeat
The iron flood

Had not our prophets cried
Ruin! No release!
And politicians lied
Predicting peace?

Now in the surging street
Sway and sweep of song
It is not death whose arm
Hurries us along

It is not death, for that
We met with a proud smile
Tossing a hand grenade
At the rocket's snarl

It is not death, but he
We feared, we fled:
Our brother, searching us –
Love's lightning tread.

III

Coming upon this face as to a map
Learning the contours not from street to street
But from the coloured ink, the gay red arteries
The yellow wrinkles and the shaded brow:
Coming to London with an eager now
The printed Golders dancing on the Green
The happy Shepherds hunting in the Bush
Coming to Chelsea and the brush
Of autumn tarnishing a square
(Whether a sheltered court, demure, austere
Or narrow alley where the children flare
Their whittled voices on the nipping air) –

Coming with guide and gift, I fell
Blundering through dark, around
No builded wall
I fell and heard my fall
Echoing through the tall
Rubble of rift and wreck
Down to the low unreaching wretched wall
Through the last door hung

On a naked nail
And the stairs flung
Up to the gap of hell:
And above, no ceiling
And below, no wall.

IV

O feet that found the way to bed,
The narrow place where prayers were said;
That danced a circle on the floor
And kicked a hollow on the door

O feet that morning noon and night
Suffered the hour to be delight
Or stood upon the edge of mist
And felt the earth, and met, and kissed –

Into the parapet of time
Memorial tower of the mind
You have ascended in a climb
Sudden as a flying bomb

You have left the city's face
Scarred and grimed by human hand
And all the magic of her map
Crumbling in brick and sand.

.   .   .   .

And though the Michaelmas is here
A mauve repose on mildewed stain
And children swing on girders grown
Rusty with the wrack of rain

And though the mushroom houses grow
In prim, prefabricated row;
Where debris was, a park will be
And here a chaste community –

Still lies the skeleton behind,
The bony manufactured grin
The voice we heard time out of mind
That rustles when the leaves are thin;

And still the footprints trace the map
Scuttle across the veins and flaws
Reverberating on the heart
To warn the way that winter was.

Bartok and the Geranium

She lifts her green umbrellas
Towards the pane
Seeking her fill of sunlight
Or of rain;
Whatever falls
She has no commentary
Accepts, extends,
Blows out her furbelows,
Her bustling boughs;

And all the while he whirls
Explodes in space,
Never content with this small room;
Not even can he be
Confined to sky
But must speed high
From galaxy to galaxy,
Wrench from the stars their momentary calm,
Stir music on the moon.

She's daylight;
He is dark.
She's heaven's held breath;
He storms and crackles
Spits with hell's own spark.

Yet in this room, this moment now
These together breathe and be:
She, essence of serenity,
He in a mad intensity
Soars beyond sight
Then hurls, lost Lucifer,
From heaven's height.
And when he's done, he's out:

She lays a lip against the glass
And preens herself in light.

Lament

What moved me, was the way your hand
Lay in my hand, not withering,
But warm, like a hand cooled in a stream
And purling still; or a bird caught in a snare
Wings folded stiff, eyes in a stare,
But still alive with the fear,
Heart hoarse with hope –
So your hand, your dead hand, my dear.

And the veins, still mounting as blue rivers,
Mounting towards the tentative finger-tips,
The delta where four seas come in –
Your fingers promontories into colourless air
Were rosy still – not chalk (like cliffs
You knew in boyhood, Isle of Wight):
But blushed with colour from the sun you sought
And muscular from garden toil;
Stained with the purple of an iris bloom,
Violas grown for a certain room;
Hands seeking faïence, filagree,
Chinese lacquer and ivory, –
Brussels lace; and a walnut piece
Carved by a hand now phosphorus.

What moved me, was the way your hand
Held life, although the pulse was gone.
The hand that carpentered a children's chair,
Carved out a stair
Held leash upon a dog in strain
Gripped wheel, swung sail,
Flicked horse's rein
And then again
Moved kings and queens meticulous on a board,
Slashed out the cards, cut bread, and poured
A purring cup of tea;
The hand so neat and nimble
Could make a tennis partner tremble,
Write a resounding round
Of sonorous verbs and nouns –
Hand that would not strike a child, and yet
Could ring a bell and send a man to doom.

And now unmoving in this Spartan room
The hand still speaks:
After the brain was fogged
And the tight lips tighter shut,
After the shy appraising eyes
Relinquished fire for the sea's green gaze –
The hand still breathes, fastens its hold on life;
Demands the whole, establishes the strife.

What moved me, was the way your hand
Lay cool in mine, not withering;
As bird still breathes, and stream runs clear –
So your hand; your dead hand, my dear.

On Looking into Henry Moore

I

Sun, stun me, sustain me
Turn me to stone:
Stone, goad me and gall me
Urge me to run.

When I have found
Passivity in fire
And fire.in stone
Female and male
I'll rise alone
Self-extending and self-known.

II

The message of the tree is this:
Aloneness is the only bliss

Self-adoration is not in it
(Narcissus tried, but could not win it)

Rather, to extend the root
Tombwards, be at home with death

But in the upper branches know
A green eternity of fire and snow.

III

The fire in the farthest hills
Is where I'd burn myself to bone:
Clad in the armour of the sun
I'd stand anew, alone.

Take off this flesh, this hasty dress
Prepare my half-self for myself:
One unit, as a tree or stone
Woman in man, and man in womb.

The Leader

II

Heaven lets down a rope
whereon I swing
the clapper of a bell
on sounding sky

And all below
they cluster with uplifted faces
black on white
and sway like flowers
to my wild clanging

Whether sun burns me
or moon rivets with steely eye
I shall ring on
till flowers are black mouths
and the stones bleed my song.

Ballad of Me

I

Misbegotten
born clumsy
bursting feet first
then topsy turvy
falling dowstairs:
the fear of
joy of
falling.

Butterfingers
father called it
throwing the ball
which catch as catch can
I couldn't.

Was it the eyes' fault
seeing the tennis net
in two places?
the ball flying, falling
space-time team-up?

What happened was:
the world, chuckling sideways
tossed me off
left me wildly
treading air
to catch up.

II

Everyone expected guilt
even I –
the pain was this:
to feel nothing.

Guilt? for the abortionist
who added one more line
to his flat perspective
one more cloud of dust
to his bleary eye?

For the child's
"onlie begetter"
who wanted a daughter?
He'll make another.

For the child herself
the abortive dancer?

No. Not for her
no tears for her
whatever she has missed
she has gained also.

III

And what fantasies do you have?
asked the psychiatrist
when I was running away from my husband.

Fantasies? fantasies?
Why surely (I might have told him)
all this living
is just that
every day dazzled
gold coins falling
     through fingers.

So I emptied my purse for the doctor
See! nothing in it
but wishes.
He sent me back home
to wash dishes.

IV

Returning further now
to childhood's *Woodlot*
I go incognito
in sandals, slacks
old sweater
and my dyed
hair

I go disarrayed
my fantasies
twist in my arms
ruffle my hair

I go wary
fearing to scare
the crow

  No one remembers Dorothy
  was ever here.

And Give Us Our Trespasses

I

Sometimes the room shakes
as the bed did shake
under love
sometimes
there's this
     earthquake.

II

As if at midnight
a socket
was plunged in the wall
and eyes sprang open.

III

Whenever I speak
     out of turn, is it?
you press your fingers
     against my mouth:
"Listen."

I hear only your heartbeat.

IV

My tongue
     is too long
my kiss
     too short
inadequate   I shrink
     from perfection.

v

Yet charged –
    your beauty charges me:

the receptor trembles

quivering water
    under the smite
      of sunlight.

vi

The telephone
    hangs on the wall
always available
    for transmitting messages:

why is it
    to lift the receiver
is to push the weight
    of a mountain?

vii

Between the impulse to speak
    and the speaking
storms crackle.

Forgive us our

    distances.

A. M. KLEIN

A. M. Klein was born in Montreal in 1909. His parents were orthodox Jews who immigrated to Canada from Europe and who saw to it that, in addition to receiving a public education, their son was instructed in the languages, texts, and commentaries of Judaism. In 1926 he enrolled at McGill and after graduating in 1929 studied law at the University of Montreal. His professional career since 1933 has been as a practising lawyer, mainly in Montreal, but he has also been involved in a variety of other activities, many of them offshoots of his Jewish heritage, such as editing the *Canadian Zionist* in the mid-thirties and the *Canadian Jewish Chronicle* during and after the war. He taught English (part-time) at McGill for a few years in the late forties (including a course in early-seventeenth-century poetry and prose). During the same years he was working on a never-to-be-completed book about Joyce, parts of which came out in *Accent* (1950) and *New Directions 13*. In 1948 he was an unsuccessful CCF candidate for the Federal Parliament.

Klein's first published poem appeared in 1929. During the thirties his work appeared frequently in *The Canadian Forum* and *New Frontier* and also in such American Jewish periodicals as *Menorah Journal* and *American Caravan*. Two long poems were reprinted in *New Provinces* (Macmillan, 1936). The material of this poetry was more often than not Judaic, but the style varied from the ornate to the blunt, from lyrical evocation to satiric social protest. In 1940 Klein published his first collection, *Hath Not a Jew* (New York: Behrman House Inc.), followed by *Poems* (Philadelphia: The Jewish Publication Society of America, 1944) and *The Hitleriad* (New York: New Directions, 1944). French-Canadians, rather than Jews, held the centre of attention in *The Rocking Chair and Other Poems* (Ryerson, 1948). As Irving Layton has put it, Klein "has a Jewish background no other writer in Canada can possibly pretend to. This made him a poet of the minorities. First he wrote about the Jew, a large enough minority; then about the French-Canadian, a slightly smaller one. Then about the Indian, a yet smaller minority. Finally he was left with the smallest of all minorities and the most persecuted – the poets" (*Teangadoir*, November, 1961). Klein's novel, *The Second Scroll* (McClelland & Stewart, 1951), which returns to his Jewish heritage in the light of the new state of Israel, includes a number of poems, but no more have appeared since 1951.

Of Kith and Kin

HEIRLOOM

My father bequeathed me no wide estates;
No keys and ledgers were my heritage;
Only some holy books with *yahrzeit* dates
Writ mournfully upon a blank front page –

Books of the Baal Shem Tov, and of his wonders;
Pamphlets upon the devil and his crew;
Prayers against road demons, witches, thunders;
And sundry other tomes for a good Jew.

Beautiful: though no pictures on them, save
The scorpion crawling on a printed track;
The Virgin floating on a scriptural wave,
Square letters twinkling in the Zodiac.

The snuff left on this page, now brown and old,
The tallow stains of midnight liturgy –
These are my coat of arms, and these unfold
My noble lineage, my proud ancestry!

And my tears, too, have stained this heirloomed ground,
When reading in these treatises some weird
Miracle, I turned a leaf and found
A white hair fallen from my father's beard.

BESTIARY

God breathe a blessing on
His small bones, every one!
The little lad, who stalks
The bible's plains and rocks
To hunt in grammar'd woods
Strange litters and wild broods;
The little lad who seeks
Beast-muzzles and bird-beaks
In cave and den and crypt,
In copse of holy script;
The little lad who looks
For quarry in holy books.

Before his eyes is born
The elusive unicorn;
There, scampering, arrive
The golden mice, the five;
Also, in antic shape,
Gay peacock and glum ape.

He hears a snort of wrath:
The fiery behemoth;
And then on biblic breeze
The crocodile's sneeze.
He sees the lion eat
Straw, and from the teat
Of tigress a young lamb
Suckling, like whelp nigh dam.

Hard by, as fleet as wind
They pass, the roe and hind,
Bravely, and with no risk,
He holds the basilisk,
Pygarg and cockatrice.
And there, most forest-wise
Among the bestiaries
The little hunter eyes
Him crawling at his leisure:
The beast Nebuchadnezzar.

MOURNERS

O, when they laved my uncle's limbs
My aunt wept bitter and long:
Who will now show my little son
The right from the wrong?
And who will sing for my delight
The holy Sabbath's song?

O, when they dug my uncle's grave,
My little cousins cried:
Who will now tell us tales about
A princess and her pride?
And who will give us pennies to
Save for a lovely bride?

Even the sparrows on the roof
Twittered their sorrow, too:
Oh, never will be thrown to us
The breadcrumbs soaked in dew;
For men have nailed him in a box,
That good little Jew.

GIFT

I will make him a little red sack
    For treasure untold,
With velvet front and a satin back,
    And braided with gold,
    His *tfillin* to hold.

I will stitch it with letters of flame,
  With square characters:
His name, and his father's name;
  And beneath it some terse
  Scriptural verse.

Yea, singing the sweet liturgy,
  He'll snare its gold cord,
Remembering me, even me,
  In the breath of his word,
  In the sight of the Lord.

The Still Small Voice

The candles splutter; and the kettle hums;
The heirloomed clock enumerates the tribes,
Upon the wine-stained table-cloth lie crumbs
Of matzoh whose wide scattering describes
Jews driven in far lands upon this earth.

The kettle hums; the candles splutter; and
Winds whispering from shutters tell re-birth
Of beauty rising in an eastern land,
Of paschal sheep driven in cloudy droves;
Of almond-blossoms colouring the breeze;
Of vineyards upon verdant terraces;
Of golden globes in orient orange-groves.
And those assembled at the table dream
Of small schemes that an April wind doth scheme,
And cry from out the sleep assailing them:
Jerusalem, next year! Next year, Jerusalem!

From *Sonnets Semitic*

II

These northern stars are scarabs in my eyes.
Not any longer can I suffer them.
I will to Palestine. We will arise
And seek the towers of Jerusalem.
Make ready to board ship. Say farewells. Con
Your Hebrew primer; supple be your tongue
To speak the crisp words baked beneath the sun,
The sinuous phrases by the sweet-singer sung.
At last, my bride, in our estate you'll wear
Sweet orange-blossoms in an orange grove.
There will be white doves fluttering in the air,
And in the meadows our contented drove,
Sheep on the hills, and in the trees, my love,
There will be sparrows twittering *Mazel Tov*.

Sonnet in Time of Affliction

The word of grace is flung from foreign thrones
And strangers lord it in the ruling-hall;
The shield of David rusts upon the wall;
The lion of Judah seeks to roar, and groans . . .
Where are the brave, the mighty? They are bones.
Bar Cochba's star has suffered its last fall.
On holy places profane spiders crawl;
The jackal leaves foul marks on temple-stones.
Ah, woe, to us, that we, the sons of peace,
Must turn our sharpened scythes to scimitars,
Must lift the hammer of the Maccabees,
Blood soak the land, make mockery of stars . . .
And woe to me, who am not one of these,
Who languish here beneath these northern stars . . .

Elijah

Elijah in a long beard
With a little staff
Hobbles through the market
And makes the children laugh.

He crows like a rooster,
He dances like a bear,
While the long-faced rabbis
Drop their jaws to stare.

He tosses his skullcap
To urchin and tot,
And catches it neatly
Right on his bald spot.

And he can tell stories
Of lovers who elope;
And terrible adventures
With cardinal and pope.

Without a single pinch, and
Without a blow or cuff,
We learned from him the Aleph,
We learned from him the Tauph.

Between the benedictions
We would play leapfrog –
O, this was a wonderful
Synagogue!

He can make a whistle
From a gander's quill;
He can make a mountain
Out of a molehill.

Oh, he is a great man!
Wished he, he could whoop
The moon down from heaven,
And roll it like a hoop;

Wished he, he could gather
The stars from the skies,
And juggle them like marbles
Before our very eyes.

Out of the Pulver
and the Polished Lens

I

The paunchy sons of Abraham
Spit on the maculate streets of Amsterdam,
Showing Spinoza, Baruch *alias* Benedict,
He and his God are under interdict.

Ah, what theology there is in spatted spittle,
And in anathema what sacred prose
Winnowing the fact from the suppose!
Indeed, what better than these two things can whittle
The scabrous heresies of Yahweh's foes,
Informing the breast where Satan gloats and crows
That saving it leave false doctrine, jot and tittle,
No vigilant thumb will leave its orthodox nose?
What better than ram's horn blown,
And candles blown out by maledictory breath,
Can bring the wanderer back to his very own,
The infidel back to his faith?

Nothing, unless it be that from the ghetto
A soldier of God advance to teach the creed,
Using as rod the irrefutable stiletto.

II

Uriel da Costa
Flightily ranted
Heresies one day,
Next day recanted.

Rabbi and bishop,
Each vies to smuggle
Soul of da Costa
Out of its struggle.

Confessional hears his
Glib paternoster;
Synagogue sees his
Penitent posture.

What is the end of
This catechism?
Bullet brings dogma
That suffers no schism.

III

Malevolent scorpions befoul thy chambers,
O my heart; they scurry across its floor,
Leaving the slimy vestiges of doubt.

Banish memento of the vermin; let
No scripture on the wall affright you; no
Ghost of da Costa; no, nor any threat.
Ignore, O heart, even as didst ignore
The bribe of florins jingling in the purse.

IV

Jehovah is factotum of the rabbis;
And Christ endures diurnal Calvary;
Polyglot God is exiled to the churches;
Synods tell God to be or not to be.

The Lord within his vacuum of heaven
Discourses his domestic policies,
With angels who break off their loud hosannas
To help him phrase infallible decrees.

Soul of Spinoza, Baruch Spinoza bids you,
Forsake the god suspended in mid-air,
Seek you that other Law, and let Jehovah
Play his game of celestial solitaire.

v

Reducing providence to theorems, the horrible atheist compiled such lore that proved, like proving two and two make four, that in the crown of God we all are gems. From glass and dust of glass he brought to light, out of the pulver and the polished lens, the prism and the flying mote; and hence the infinitesimal and infinite.

Is it a marvel, then, that he forsook the abracadabra of the synagogue, and holding with timelessness a duologue, deciphered a new scripture in the book? Is it a marvel that he left old fraud for passion intellectual of God?

VI

Unto the crown of bone cry *Suzerain!*
Do genuflect before the jewelled brain!
Lavish the homage of the vassal; let
The blood grow heady with strong epithet;
O cirque of the Cabbalist! O proud skull!
Of alchemy. O crucible!
Sanctum sanctorum; grottoed hermitage
Where sits the bearded sage!
O golden bowl of Koheleth! and of fate
O hourglass within the pate!
Circling, O planet in the occiput!
O Macrocosm, sinew-shut!
Yea, and having uttered this loud *Te Deum*
Ye have been singularly dumb.

VII

I am weak before the wind; before the sun
    I faint; I lose my strength;
I am utterly vanquished by a star;
    I go to my knees, at length

Before the song of a bird; before
    The breath of spring or fall
I am lost; before these miracles
    I am nothing at all.

VIII

Lord, accept my hallelujahs; look not askance at these my petty words; unto perfection a fragment makes its prayer.

For thou art the world, and I am part thereof; thou art the blossom and I its fluttering petal.

I behold thee in all things, and in all things: lo, it is myself; I look into the pupil of thine eye, it is my very countenance I see.

Thy glory fills the earth; it is the earth; the noise of the deep, the moving of many waters, is it not thy voice aloud, O Lord, aloud that all may hear?

The wind through the almond-trees spreads the fragrance of thy robes; the turtle-dove twittering utters diminutives of thy love; at the rising of the sun I behold thy countenance.

Yea, and in the crescent moon, thy little finger's finger-nail.

If I ascend up into heaven, thou art there; If I make my bed in hell, behold thou art there.

Thou art everywhere; a pillar to thy sanctuary is every blade of grass.

Wherefore I said to the wicked, Go to the ant, thou sluggard, seek thou an audience with God.

On the swift wings of a star, even on the numb legs of a snail, thou dost move, O Lord.

A babe in swaddling clothes laughs at the sunbeams on the door's lintel, the sucklings play with thee; with thee Kopernik holds communion through a lens.

I am thy son, O Lord, and brother to all that lives am I.

The flowers of the field, they are kith and kin to me; the lily my sister, the rose is my blood and flesh.

Even as the stars in the firmament move, so does my inward heart, and even as the moon draws the tides in the bay, so does it the blood in my veins.

For thou art the world, and I am part thereof;

Howbeit, even in dust I am resurrected; and even in decay I live again.

IX

Think of Spinoza, then, not as you think
Of Shabbathai Zvi who for a time of life
Took to himself the Torah for a wife,
And underneath the silken canopy
Made public: Thou art hallowed unto me.

Think of Spinoza, rather, plucking tulips
Within the garden of Mynheer, forgetting
Dutchmen and Rabbins, and consumptive fretting,
Plucking his tulips in the Holland sun,
Remembering the thought of the Adored,
Spinoza, gathering flowers for the One,
The ever-unwedded lover of the Lord.

Design for Mediaeval Tapestry

Somewhere a hungry muzzle rooted.
The frogs among the sedges croaked.
Into the night a screech-owl hooted.

A clawed mouse squeaked and struggled, choked.
The wind pushed antlers through the bushes.
Terror stalked through the forest, cloaked.

Was it a robber broke the bushes?
Was it a knight in armoured thews,
Walking in mud, and bending rushes?

Was it a provost seeking Jews?
The Hebrews shivered; their teeth rattled;
Their beards glittered with gelid dews.

Gulped they their groans, for silence tattled;
They crushed their sighs, for quiet heard;
They had their thoughts on Israel battled

By pagan and by Christian horde.
They moved their lips in pious anguish.
They made no sound. They never stirred.

*   *   *

REB ZADOC HAS MEMORIES

Reb Zadoc's brain is a German town:
Hermits come from lonely grottos
Preaching the right for Jews to drown;

Soldiers who vaunt their holy mottos
Stroking the cross that is a sword;
Barons plotting in cabal sottos;

A lady spitting on the abhorred.
The market-place and faggot-fire –
A hangman burning God's true word;

A clean-shaved traitor-Jew; a friar
Dropping his beads upon his paunch;
The heavens speared by a Gothic spire;

The Judengasse and its stench
Rising from dark and guarded alleys
Where Jew is neighbored to harlot-wench

Perforce ecclesiastic malice;
The exile-booths of Jacob where
Fat burghers come to pawn a chalice

While whistling a Jew-hating air;
Peasants regarding Jews and seeking
The hooves, the tail, the horn-crowned hair;

And target for a muddy streaking,
The yellow badge upon the breast,
The vengeance of a papal wreaking;

The imposts paid for this fine crest;
Gay bailiffs serving writs of seizure;
Even the town fool and his jest –

Stroking his beard with slowly leisure,
A beard that was but merely down,
Rubbing his palms with gloating pleasure,

Counting fictitious crown after crown.
Reb Zadoc's brain is a torture-dungeon;
Reb Zadoc's brain is a German town.

REB DANIEL SHOCHET REFLECTS

The toad seeks out its mud; the mouse discovers
The nibbled hole; the sparrow owns its nest;
About the blind mole earthy shelter hovers.

The louse avows the head where it is guest;
Even the roach calls some dark fent his dwelling.
But Israel owns a sepulchre, at best.

NAHUM-THIS-ALSO-IS-FOR-THE-GOOD PONDERS

The wrath of God is just. His punishment
Is most desirable. The flesh of Jacob
Implores the scourge. For this was Israel meant.

Below we have no life. But we will wake up
Beyond, where popes will lave our feet, where princes
Will heed our insignificantest hiccup.

The sins of Israel only blood-shed rinses.
We teach endurance. Lo, we are not spent.
We die, we live; at once we are three tenses.

Our skeletons are bibles; flesh is rent
Only to prove a thesis, stamp a moral.
The rack prepared: for this was Israel meant.

ISAIAH EPICURE AVERS

Seek reasons; rifle your theology;
Philosophize; expend your dialectic;
Decipher and translate God's diary;

Discover causes, primal and eclectic;
I cannot; all I know is this:
That pain doth render flesh most sore and hectic;

That lance-points prick; the scorched bones hiss;
That thumbscrews agonize, and that a martyr
Is mad if he considers these things bliss.

JOB REVILES

God is grown ancient. He no longer hears.
He has been deafened by his perfect thunders.
With clouds for cotton he has stopped his ears.

The Lord is purblind; and his heaven sunders
Him from the peccadillos of this earth.
He meditates his youth; he dreams; he wonders.

His cherubs have acquired beards and girth.
They cannot move to do his bidding. Even
The angels yawn. Satan preserves his mirth.

How long, O Lord, will Israel's heart be riven?
How long will we cry to a dotard God
To let us keep the breath that He has given?

How long will you sit on your throne, and nod?

JUDITH MAKES COMPARISONS

Judith had heard a troubadour
Singing beneath a castle-turret
Of truth, chivàlry, and honoùr,
Of virtue, and of gallant merit, –
Judith had heard a troubadour
Lauding the parfait knightly spirit,
Singing beneath the ivied wall.
The cross-marked varlet Judith wrestled
Was not like these at all, at all . . .

EZEKIEL THE SIMPLE OPINES

If we will fast for forty days; if we
Will read the psalms thrice over; if we offer
To God some blossom-bursting litany,

And to the poor a portion of the coffer;
If we don sack-cloth, and let ashes rain
Upon our heads, despite the boor and scoffer,

Certes, these things will never be again.

SOLOMON TALMUDI CONSIDERS HIS LIFE

Rather that these blood-thirsty pious vandals,
Bearing sable in heart, and gules on arm,
Had made me ready for the cerement-candles,

Than that they should have taken my one charm
Against mortality, my exegesis:
The script that gave the maggot the alarm.

Jews would have crumpled Rashi's simple thesis
On reading this, and Ibn Ezra's version;
Maimonides they would have torn to pieces.

For here, in black and white, by God's conversion,
I had plucked secrets from the pentateuch,
And gathered strange arcana from dispersion,

The essence and quintessence of the book!
Green immortality smiled out its promise—
I hung my gaberdine on heaven's hook.

Refuting Duns, and aquinatic Thomas,
Confounding Moslems, proving the one creed
A simple sentence broken by no commas,

I thought to win myself eternal meed,
I thought to move the soul with sacred lever
And lift the heart to God in very deed.

Ah, woe is me, and to my own endeavour,
That on that day they burned my manuscript,
And lost my name, for certain, and for ever!

SIMEON TAKES HINTS FROM HIS ENVIRONS

Heaven is God's grimace at us on high.
This land is a cathedral; speech, its sermon.
The moon is a rude gargoyle in the sky.

The leaves rustle. Come, who will now determine
Whether this be the wind, or priestly robes.
The frogs croak out ecclesiastic German,

Whereby our slavish ears have punctured lobes.
The stars are mass-lamps on a lofty altar;
Even the angels are Judaeophobes.

There is one path; in it I shall not falter.
Let me rush to the bosom of the state
And church, grasp lawyer-code and monkish psalter,

And being Christianus Simeon, late
Of Jewry, have much comfort and salvation –
Salvation in this life, at any rate.

ESTHER HEARS ECHOES OF HIS VOICE

How sweetly did he sing grace after meals!
He now is silent. He has fed on sorrow.
He lies where he is spurned by faithless heels.

His voice was honey. Lovers well might borrow
Warmth from his words. His words were musical,
Making the night so sweet, so sweet the morrow!

Can I forget the tremors of his call?
Can kiddush benediction be forgotten?
His blood is spilled like wine. The earth is sharp with gall.

As soothing as the promises begotten
Of penitence and love; as lovely as
The turtle-dove; as soft as snow in cotton,

Whether he lulled a child or crooned the laws,
And sacred as the eighteen prayers, so even
His voice. His voice was so. His voice that was . . .

      *   *   *

The burgher sleeps beside his wife, and dreams
Of human venery, and Hebrew quarry.
His sleep contrives him many little schemes.

There will be Jews, dead, moribund and gory;
There will be booty; there will be dark maids,
And there will be a right good spicy story . . .

      *   *   *

The moon has left her vigil. Lucifer fades.
Whither shall we betake ourselves, O Father?
Whither to flee? And where to find our aids?

The wrath of people is like foam and lather,
Risen against us. Wherefore, Lord, and why?
The winds assemble; the cold and hot winds gather

To scatter us. They do not heed our cry.
The sun rises and leaps the red horizon,
And like a bloodhound swoops across the sky.

From *Greetings On This Day*

I

Lest grief clean out the sockets of your eyes,
Lest anguish purge your heart of happiness,
Lest you go shaking fists at passive skies,
And mouthing blasphemies in your distress,

Be silent. Sorrow is a leper; shun
The presence of his frosted phantom. Plant
Small stones for eyes so that no tears may run;
And underneath your ribs set adamant.

II

O Chronicler, pull down the heavy tome;
   Open a blank page, fashion a pen from bone;
Dip it in skulls where blood is ink; inscribe
The welcome Jews received on coming home.

Omit your adjectives, sad Jeremiah,
Spare you your adverbs; let your phrases house
No too-protesting tenant of despair;
And if the meager tale brings no Messiah,
Messiah is a short conspiracy
   Of throat and air.

Ballad of the Days of the Messiah

I

O the days of the Messiah are at hand, are at hand!
   The days of the Messiah are at hand!
I can hear the air-raid siren, blow away the age of iron,
   Blast away the age of iron
   That was builded on the soft quick-sand.
O the days of the Messiah are at hand!

II

O Leviathan is ready for the feed, for the feed!
   Leviathan is ready for the feed!
And I hold firm to the credo that both powder and torpedo
   Have so fried that good piscedo
He is ready for the eating, scale and seed!
   Leviathan is ready for the feed!

III

Yes, the sacred wine is ready for the good, for the good,
   The wine of yore intended for the good –
Only all that ruddy water has now turned to blood and slaughter
   Has fermented into slaughter,
Aged for so long, as it has been, in the wood –
   That wine of yore intended for the good!

IV

O I see him falling! Will he shoot? Will he shoot?
   Will Messiah's falling herald aim and shoot?
'Tis, Elijah, he announces, as he falls from sky, and bounces
   Out of all those silken flounces
Of the heaven-sent and colored parachute:
   Messiah, he is coming, and won't shoot!

v

Don't you hear Messiah coming in his tank, in his tank?
   Messiah in an armor-metalled tank?
I can see the pillared fire, speeding on the metal tire
   Over muck and out of mire
And the seraphim a-shooting from its flank!
   O Messiah, he stands grimy in his tank!

Psalm IV

*A psalm of Abraham, touching
his green pastures:*

From pastures green, whereon I lie,
Beside still waters, far from crowds,
I lift hosannahs to the sky
And hallelujahs to the clouds,

Only to see where clouds should sit,
And in that space the sky should fill,
The fierce carnivorous Messerschmidt,
The Heinkel on the kill.

They'll not be green for very long,
Those pastures of my peace, nor will
The heavens be a place for song,
Nor the still waters still.

Psalm XII

*To the chief musician, who played
for the dancers:*

These were the ones who thanked their God
With dancing jubilant shins:
The beggar, who for figleaf pride
Sold shoelaces and pins;
The blindman for his brotherly dog;
The cripple for his chair;
The mauled one for the blessed gasp
Of the cone of sweet kind air.
I did not see this dance, but men
Have praised its grace; yet I
Still cannot fathom how they danced,
Or why.

Psalm XXVII

A psalm to teach humility:

O sign and wonder of the barnyard, more
beautiful than the pheasant, more melodious
than nightingale! O creature marvellous!

Prophet of sunrise, and foreteller of times!
Vizier of the constellations! Sage,
red-bearded, scarlet-turbaned, in whose brain
the stars lie scattered like well-scattered grain!

Calligraphist upon the barnyard page!
Five-noted balladist! Crower of rhymes!

O morning-glory mouth, O throat of dew,
announcing the out-faring of the blue,
the greying and the going of the night,
the coming on,
the imminent coming of the dawn,
the coming of the kinsmen, the brightly-plumaged sun!

O creature marvellous – and O blessed Creator,
Who givest to the rooster wit
to know the movements of the turning day,
to understand, to herald it,
better than I, who neither sing nor crow
and of the sun's goings and comings nothing know.

Psalm XXVIII

*A psalm or prayer – praying his
portion with beasts:*

The better to understand Thy ways,
Divinity I would divine,
Let me companion all my days
The more-than-human beasts of Thine;

The sheep whose little woolly throat
Taught the child Isaac sacrifice;
The dove returning to Noah's boat,
Sprigless, and with tearful eyes;

The ass instructing Balaam
The discourse of inspired minds;
And David's lost and bleating lamb,
And Solomon's fleet lovely hinds;

Enfold me in their fold, and let
Me learn their mystic parables –
Of food that desert ravens set,
And of the lion's honeyed fells.

Above all, teach me blessedness
Of him, Azazel, that dear goat,
Sent forth into the wilderness
To hallow it with one sad note.

Psalm XXXII

A song that the ships of Jaffa
did sing in the night:

The ship leaves Jaffa, treasure in its hold:
Figs, coronets of sweetness; sweeter dates;
Citrons, like perfume phials, packed in crates;
Boxed oranges, the scented globes of gold;
Grape clusters, and wine bottles, dusty, old;
Sweet almonds, toothsomest of delicates;
Bleeding golgothas of red pomegranates;
All smooth and fresh, and innocent of mould.
And Torah scrolls penned by some scribe, now dead,
And pray'r-shawls woven in an eastern loom,
And palm-leaves shipped to the Uncomforted,
And candlesticks to light some Sabbath gloom.
And little sacks of holy earth to spread
Under a pious skull in a far tomb . . .

Psalm XXXV

A psalm of Abraham, which he made
because of fear in the night:

Thou settest them about my bed,
The four good angels of the night,
Invisible wings on left and right,
An holy watch at foot and head:

Gabriel, Uriel, Raphael,
And Michael, of the angelic host
Who guard my sleep-entrusted ghost
Until day break, and break the spell.

Until day break, and shadows pass
My bones lie in a sack of flesh,
My blood lies caught in carmined mesh,
And I am wholly trodden grass.

But those the warders of life and limb
Escort my soul to distant shores,
My soul that in its dreaming soars
With seraphim and cherubim,

To lands unrecognized, to shores
Bright with great sunlight, musical
With singing of such scope and skill,
It is too much for human ears.

I see the angel's drinking-cup,
That flower that so scents the air!
The golden domes! The towers there!
My mind could never think them up!

Yet when the shadows flee away,
And fly the four good angels, and
I fare forth, exiled from that land,
Back to my blood, my bone, my day,

Untowered, unflowered, unscented banks,
Back to the lumpy sack of skin,
The head, the torso, and the shin,
I offer up, to Thee, my thanks.

From *The Hitleriad*

Heil heavenly muse, since also thou must be
Like my song's theme, a sieg-heil'd deity,
Be with me now, but not as once, for song:
Not odes do I indite, indicting Wrong!
Be with me, for I fall from grace to sin,
Spurning this day thy proffered hippocrene,
To taste the poison'd lager of Berlin!

Happier would I be with other themes—
(Who rallies nightmares when he could have dreams?)
With other themes, and subjects more august—
Adolf I sing but only since I must.
I must! Shall I continue the sweet words
That praise the blossoming flowers, the blossoming birds,
While, afar off, I hear the stamping herds?
Shall I, within my ivory tower, sit
And play the solitaire of rhyme and wit,
While Indignation pounds upon the door,
And Pity sobs, until she sobs no more,
And, in the woods, there yelp the hounds of war?

I am the grandson of the prophets! I
Shall not seal lips against iniquity.
Let anger take me in its grasp; let hate,
Hatred of evil prompt me, and dictate!
And let the world see that swastika-stain,
That heart, where no blood is, but high octane,
That little brain—
So that once seen the freak be known again!
Oh, even as his truncheon'd crimes are wrought,
And while the spilt blood is still body-hot,
And even as his doom still seems in doubt,
Let deeds unspeakable be spoken out.

The Sugaring

For Guy Sylvestre

Starved, scarred, lenten, amidst ash of air,
roped and rough-shirted, the maples in the unsheltered grove
after their fasts and freezings stir.
Ah, winter for each one,
each gospel tree, each saint of the calendar,
has been a penance, a purchase: the nails of ice!
wind's scourge! the rooted cross!
Nor are they done with the still stances of love,
the fiery subzeros of sacrifice.

For standing amidst the thorns of their own bones,
eased by the tombs' coolth of resurrection time,–
the pardon, the purgatorial groans
almost at bitter end,
but not at end–the carving auger runs
spiral the round stigmata through each limb!
The saints bleed down their sides!
And look! men catch this juice of their agonized prime
to boil in kettles the sap of seraphim!

O, out of this calvary Canadian comes bliss,
savour and saving images of holy things,
a sugared metamorphosis!
Ichor of dulcitude
shaping sweet relics, crystalled spotlessness!
And the pious pour into the honeyed dies
the sacred hearts, the crowns,
thanking those saints for syrops of their dying
and blessing the sweetness of their sacrifice.

Krieghoff: Calligrammes

Let the blank whiteness of this page be snow
and majuscule the make of Cornelius:
    then tented A's inverted V's
may circumflex and shade the paysage page
    with French-Canadian trees;
or equal the arrows of the frozen flow
    by the last minus of degrees
stopped in their flight; or show
the wigwams and the gables—
of Krieghoff the pat petted verities.

And any signs will do:
the ladder H that prongs above the chimney;
prone J's on which the gay sleighs run;
the Q and her papoose:
crucifix Y; or bosomed farmwife B—
wanting an easel and the painter's flourish
with alphabet make free,
make squares, make curlecues
of his simplicity.

But colours? Ah, the two colours!

These must be spun, these must be bled
out of the iris of the intent sight:
red rufous roseate crimson russet red
    blank candid white.

Political Meeting

(For Camillien Houde)

On the school platform, draping the folding seats,
they wait the chairman's praise and glass of water.
Upon the wall the agonized Y initials their faith.

Here all are laic; the skirted brothers have gone.
Still, their equivocal absence is felt, like a breeze
that gives curtains the sounds of surplices.

The hall is yellow with light, and jocular;
suddenly some one lets loose upon the air
the ritual bird which the crowd in snares of singing

catches and plucks, throat, wings, and little limbs.
Fall the feathers of sound, like *alouette's*.
The chairman, now, is charming, full of asides and wit,

building his orators, and chipping off
the heckling gargoyles popping in the hall.
(Outside, in the dark, the street is body-tall,

flowered with faces intent on the scarecrow thing
that shouts to thousands the echoing
of their own wishes.) The Orator has risen!

Worshipped and loved, their favourite visitor,
a country uncle with sunflower seeds in his pockets,
full of wonderful moods, tricks, imitative talk,

he is their idol: like themselves, not handsome,
not snobbish, not of the *Grande Allee! Un homme!*
Intimate, informal, he makes bear's compliments

to the ladies; is gallant; and grins;
goes for the balloon, his opposition, with pins;
jokes also on himself, speaks of himself

in the third person, slings slang, and winks with folklore:
and knows now that he has them, kith and kin.
Calmly, therefore, he begins to speak of war,

praises the virtue of being *Canadien*,
of being at peace, of faith, of family,
and suddenly his other voice: *Where are your sons?*

He is tearful, choking tears; but not he
would blame the clever English; in their place
he'd do the same; maybe.

Where *are* your sons?
                            The whole street wears one face,
shadowed and grim; and in the darkness rises
the body-odour of race.

Monsieur Gaston

You remember the big Gaston, for whom everyone predicted
a bad end? –
Gaston, the neighbour's gossip and his mother's cross?
You remember him *vaurien*, always out of a job,
with just enough clinking coinage
for pool, bright neckties, and blondes, –
the scented Gaston in the poolroom lolling
in meadows of green baize?
In clover now. Through politics. *Monsieur* Gaston.

They say the Minister of a certain department does not move
without him; and they say, to make it innocent, –
chauffeur.
But everyone understands. Why, wherever our Gaston smiles
a nightclub rises and the neons flash.
To his slightest whisper
the bottled rye, like a fawning pet-dog, gurgles.
The burlesque queen will not undress
unless Monsieur Gaston says yes.
And the Madame will shake her hand behind the curtain-rods
unless he nods.

A changed man, Gaston; almost a civil servant,
keeps records, appointments, women; speaks tough English;
is very much respected.
You should hear with what greetings his distinguished approach
    is greeted;
you should see the gifts he gets,
with compliments for his season.

The Cripples

(Oratoire de St. Joseph)

Bundled their bones, upon the ninety-nine stairs—
St. Joseph's ladder—the knobs of penance come;
the folded cripples counting up their prayers.

How rich, how plumped with blessing is that dome!
The gourd of Brother André! His sweet days
rounded! Fulfilled! Honeyed to honeycomb!

whither the hands, upon the ninety-nine trays,
the palsied, who double their aspen selves, the lame,
the unsymmetrical, the dead-limbed, raise

their look, their hope, and the *idée fixe* of their maim,—
knowing the surgery's in the heart. Are not
the ransomed crutches worshippers? And the fame

of the brother sanatorial to this plot?—
God mindful of the sparrows on the stairs?
Yes, to their faith this mountain of stairs, is not!

They know, they know, that suddenly their cares
and orthopedics will fall from them, and they
stand whole again.

        Roll empty away, wheelchairs,
and crutches, without armpits, hop away!

And I who in my own faith once had faith like this,
but have not now, am crippled more than they.

Montreal

I

O city metropole, isle riverain!
Your ancient pavages and sainted routs
Traverse my spirit's conjured avenues!
Splendor erablic of your promenades
Foliates there, and there your maisonry
Of pendent balcon and escalier'd march,
Unique midst English habitat,
Is vivid Normandy!

II

You populate the pupils of my eyes:
Thus, does the Indian, plumèd, furtivate
Still through your painted autumns, Ville-Marie!
Though palisades have passed, though calumet
With tabac of your peace enfumes the air,
Still do I spy the phantom, aquiline,
Genuflect, moccasin'd, behind
His statue in the square!

III

Thus, costumed images before me pass,
Haunting your archives architectural:
Coureur de bois, in posts where pelts were portaged;
Seigneur within his candled manoir; Scot
Ambulant through his bank, pillar'd and vast.
Within your chapels, voyaged mariners
Still pray, and personage departed,
All present from your past!

VI

Grand port of navigations, multiple
The lexicons uncargo'd at your quays,
Sonnant though strange to me; but chiefest, I,
Auditor of your music, cherish the
Joined double-melodied vocabulaire
Where English vocable and roll Ecossic,
Mollified by the parle of French
Bilinguefact your air!

V

Such your suaver voice, hushed Hochelaga!
But for me also sound your potencies,
Fortissimos of sirens fluvial,
Bruit of manufactory, and thunder
From foundry issuant, all puissant tone
Implenishing your hebdomad; and then
Sanct silence, and your argent belfries
Clamant in orison!

VI

You are a part of me, O all your quartiers—
And of dire pauvrete and of richesse—
To finished time my homage loyal claim;
You are locale of infancy, milieu
Vital of institutes that formed my fate;
And you above the city, scintillant,
Mount Royal, are my spirit's mother,
Almative, poitrinate!

VII

Never do I sojourn in alien place
But I do languish for your scenes and sounds,
City of reverie, nostalgic isle,
Pendant most brilliant on Laurentian cord!
The coigns of your boulevards—my signiory—
Your suburbs are my exile's verdure fresh,
Your parks, your fountain'd parks—
Pasture of memory!

VIII

City, O city, you are vision'd as
A parchemin roll of saecular exploit
Inked with the script of eterne souvenir!
You are in sound, chanson and instrument!
Mental, you rest forever edified
With tower and dome; and in these beating valves,
Here in these beating valves, you will
For all my mortal time reside!

Grain Elevator

Up from the low-roofed dockyard warehouses
it rises blind and babylonian
like something out of legend. Something seen
in a children's coloured book. Leviathan
swamped on our shore? The cliffs of some other river?
The blind ark lost and petrified? A cave
built to look innocent, by pirates? Or
some eastern tomb a travelled patron here makes local?

But even when known, it's more than what it is:
for here, as in a Josephdream, bow down
the sheaves, the grains, the scruples of the sun
garnered for darkness; and Saskatchewan
is rolled like a rug of a thick and golden thread.
O prison of prairies, ship in whose galleys roll
sunshines like so many shaven heads,
waiting the bushel-burst out of the beached bastille!

Sometimes, it makes me think Arabian,
the grain picked up, like tic-tacs out of time:
first one; an other; singly, one by one; –
to save life. Sometimes, some other races claim
the twinship of my thought, – as the river stirs
restless in a white Caucasian sleep,
or, as in the steerage of the elevators,
the grains, Mongolian and crowded, dream.

A box: cement, hugeness, and rightangles –
merely the sight of it leaning in my eyes
mixes up continents and makes a montage
of inconsequent time and uncontiguous space.
It's because it's bread. It's because
bread is its theme, an absolute. Because
always this great box flowers over us
with all the coloured faces of mankind . . .

Frigidaire

Even in July it is our winter corner,
hill 70 of our kitchen, rising white
and cool to the eye, cool to the alpenfinger.
The shadows and wind of snowfall fall from its sides.

And when the door swings away, like a cloud blown,
the village is Laurentian, tiered and bright,
with thresholds of red, white roofs, and scattered greens;
and it has a sky, and clouds, and a northern light.

Is peopled. On its vallied streets there stands
a bevy of milk, coifed like the sisters of snow;
and beaded bosoms of butter; and red farmhands;
all poised, as if to hear from the distant meadow,

there on the heights, with its little flowers of white,
the cubes that seem to sound like pasture bells.
Fixed to that far-off tingle they don't quite
hear. they stand, frozen with eavesdropping, like icicles.

And there on the heights, the storm's electric, thriving
with muffled thunder, and lightning slow and white!
It is a private sky, a weather exclusive,
a slow, sensational, and secret sight.

Lone Bather

Upon the ecstatic diving board the diver,
poised for parabolas, lets go
lets go his manshape to become a bird.
Is bird, and topsy-turvy
the pool floats overhead, and the white tiles snow
their crazy hexagons. Is dolphin. Then
is plant with lilies bursting from his heels.

Himself, suddenly mysterious and marine,
bobs up a merman leaning on his hills.

Plashes and plays alone the deserted pool;
as those, is free, who think themselves unseen.
He rolls in his heap of fruit,
he slides his belly over
the melonrinds of water, curved and smooth and green.
Feels good: and trains, like little acrobats
his echoes dropping from the galleries;
circles himself over a rung of water;
swims fancy and gay; taking a notion, hides
under the satins of his great big bed, –
and then comes up to float until he thinks
the ceiling at his brow, and nowhere any sides.

His thighs are a shoal of fishes: scattered: he
turns with many gloves of greeting
towards the sunnier water and the tiles.

Upon the tiles he dangles from his toes
lazily the eight reins of his ponies.

An afternoon, far from the world
a street sound throws like a stone, with paper, through the glass.
Up, he is chipped enamel, grained with hair.
The gloss of his footsteps follows him to the showers,
the showers, and the male room, and the towel
which rubs the bird, the plant, the dolphin back again
personable plain.

Portrait of the Poet as Landscape

I

Not an editorial-writer, bereaved with bartlett,
mourns him, the shelved Lycidas.
No actress squeezes a glycerine tear for him.
The radio broadcast lets his passing pass.
And with the police, no record. Nobody, it appears,
either under his real name or his alias,
missed him enough to report.

It is possible that he is dead, and not discovered.
It is possible that he can be found some place
in a narrow closet, like the corpse in a detective story,
standing, his eyes staring, and ready to fall on his face.
It is also possible that he is alive
and amnesiac, or mad, or in retired disgrace,
or beyond recognition lost in love.

We are sure only that from our real society
he has disappeared; he simply does not count,
except in the pullulation of vital statistics—
somebody's vote, perhaps, an anonymous taunt
of the Gallup poll, a dot in a government table—
but not felt, and certainly far from eminent—
in a shouting mob, somebody's sigh.

O, he who unrolled culture from his scroll—
the prince's quote, the rostrum-rounding roar—
who under one name made articulate
heaven, and under another the seven-circled air,
is, if he is at all, a number, an x,
a Mr. Smith in a hotel register,—
incognito, lost, lacunal.

II

The truth is he's not dead, but only ignored—
like the mirroring lenses forgotten on a brow
that shine with the guilt of their unnoticed world.
The truth is he lives among neighbours, who, though they will allow
him a passable fellow, think him eccentric, not solid,
a type that one can forgive, and for that matter, forego.

Himself he has his moods, just like a poet.
Sometimes, depressed to nadir, he will think all lost,
will see himself as throwback, relict, freak,
his mother's miscarriage, his great-grandfather's ghost,
and he will curse his quintuplet senses, and their tutors
in whom he put, as he should not have put, his trust.

Then he will remember his travels over that body –
the torso verb, the beautiful face of the noun,
and all those shaped and warm auxiliaries!
A first love it was, the recognition of his own.
Dear limbs adverbial, complexion of adjective,
dimple and dip of conjugation!

And then remember how this made a change in him
affecting for always the glow and growth of his being;
how suddenly was aware of the air, like shaken tinfoil,
of the patents of nature, the shock of belated seeing,
the loneliness peering from the eyes of crowds;
the integers of thought; the cube-roots of feeling.

Thus, zoomed to zenith, sometimes he hopes again,
and sees himself as a character, with a rehearsed role:
the Count of Monte Cristo, come for his revenges;
the unsuspected heir, with papers; the risen soul;
or the chloroformed prince awaking from his flowers;
or – deflated again – the convict on parole.

III

He is alone; yet not completely alone.
Pins on a map of a colour similar to his,
each city has one, sometimes more than one;
here, caretakers of art, in colleges;
in offices, there, with arm-bands, and green-shaded;
and there, pounding their catalogued beats in libraries, –

everywhere menial, a shadow's shadow.
And always for their egos – their outmoded art.
Thus, having lost the bevel in the ear,
they know neither up nor down, mistake the part
for the whole, curl themselves in a comma,
talk technics, make a colon their eyes. They distort –

such is the pain of their frustration—truth
to something convolute and cerebral.
How they do fear the slap of the flat of the platitude!
Now Pavlov's victims, their mouths water at bell,
the platter empty.
                    See they set twenty-one jewels
into their watches; the time they do not tell!

Some, patagonian in their own esteem,
and longing for the multiplying word,
join party and wear pins, now have a message,
an ear, and the convention-hall's regard.
Upon the knees of ventriloquists, they own,
of their dandled brightness, only the paint and board.

And some go mystical, and some go mad.
One stares at a mirror all day long, as if
to recognize himself; another courts
angels,—for here he does not fear rebuff;
and a third, alone, and sick with sex, and rapt,
doodles him symbols convex and concave.

O schizoid solitudes! O purities
curdling upon themselves! Who live for themselves,
or for each other, but for nobody else;
desire affection, private and public loves;
are friendly, and then quarrel and surmise
the secret perversions of each other's lives.

IV

He suspects that something has happened, a law
been passed, a nightmare ordered. Set apart,
he finds himself, with special haircut and dress,
as on a reservation. Introvert.
He does not understand this; sad conjecture
muscles and palls thrombotic on his heart.

He thinks an impostor, having studied his personal biography,
his gestures, his moods, now has come forward to pose
in the shivering vacuums his absence leaves.
Wigged with his laurel, that other, and faked with his face,
he pats the heads of his children, pecks his wife,
and is at home, and slippered, in his house.

So he guesses at the impertinent silhouette
that talks to his phone-piece and slits open his mail.
Is it the local tycoon who for a hobby
plays poet, he so epical in steel?
The orator, making a pause? Or is that man
he who blows his flash of brass in the jittering hall?

Or is he cuckolded by the troubadour
rich and successful out of celluloid?
Or by the don who unrhymes atoms? Or
the chemist death built up? Pride, lost impostor'd pride,
it is another, another, whoever he is,
who rides where he should ride.

V

Fame, the adrenalin: to be talked about;
to be a verb; to be introduced as *The:*
to smile with endorsement from slick paper; make
caprices anecdotal; to nod to the world; to see
ones name like a song upon the marquees played;
to be forgotten with embarrassment; to be –
to be.

It has its attractions, but is not the thing;
nor is it the ape mimesis who speaks from the tree
ancestral; nor the merkin joy . . .
Rather it is stark infelicity
which stirs him from his sleep, undressed, asleep
to walk upon roofs and window-sills and defy
the gape of gravity.

VI

Therefore he seeds illusions. Look, he is
the nth Adam taking a green inventory
in world but scarcely uttered, naming, praising,
the flowering fiats in the meadow, the
syllabled fur, stars aspirate, the pollen
whose sweet collision sounds eternally.
For to praise

the world – he, solitary man – is breath
to him. Until it has been praised, that part
has not been. Item by exciting item –
air to his lungs, and pressured blood to his heart. –
they are pulsated, and breathed, until they map,
not the world's, but his own body's chart!

And now in imagination he has climbed
another planet, the better to look
with single camera view upon this earth –
its total scope, and each afflated tick,
its talk, its trick, its tracklessness – and this,
this he would like to write down in a book!

To find a new function for the declassé craft
archaic like the fletcher's; to make a new thing;
to say the word that will become sixth sense;
perhaps by necessity and indirection bring
new forms to life, anonymously, new creeds –
O, somehow pay back the daily larcenies of the lung!

These are not mean ambitions. It is already something
merely to entertain them. Meanwhile, he
makes of his status as zero a rich garland,
a halo of his anonymity,
and lives alone, and in his secret shines
like phosphorus. At the bottom of the sea.

NOTE

ON THE BIOGRAPHIES

In preparing the biographical headpieces, I was particularly indebted to the information available in Desmond Pacey's *Ten Canadian Poets* (Ryerson, 1958) and his introduction to Dorothy Livesay's *Selected Poems* (Ryerson, 1957).

NOTE

ON THE TEXT

E. J. PRATT. "The Great Feud" appeared in *Titans* (1926), "The Highway" in *Many Moods* (1932), "Come Away, Death" and "The Truant" in *Still Life and Other Verse* (1943) and *Towards the Last Spike* in its titular volume (1952). The texts are reprinted from the *Collected Poems* (1958).

A. J. M. SMITH. The first sixteen poems appeared in *News of the Phoenix* (1943), the next eight in *A Sort of Ecstasy* (1954) and the rest in the *Collected Poems* (1962). The texts for all thirty-one are reprinted from the *Collected Poems*.

F. R. SCOTT. The first eleven poems appeared in *Overture* (1945), the next eight in *Events and Signals* (1954), the next three in *The Eye of the Needle* (1957) and the last six in *Signature* (1964). The texts for all twenty eight are reprinted from the *Selected Poems* (1966), except for "The Bartail Cock" from *Signature*.

DOROTHY LIVESAY. The first two poems appeared in *Green Pitcher* (1928), the next six in *Signpost* (1932), the next five in *Day and Night* (1944), the next four in *Poems for People* (1947), the next one in *New Poems* (1955), the next two in the *Selected Poems* (1957), the next one in *The Colour of God's Face* (1964) and the last two in *The Canadian Forum* (January, 1965 and June, 1966). The texts are all reprinted from the *Selected Poems* except for numbers 2, 3, 4, 8, 16, 21, 22, 23, which are reprinted from the above sources.

A. M. KLEIN. The first eight poems appeared in *Hath Not a Jew* (1940), the next seven in *Poems* (1944), the next one in *The Hitleriad* (1944) and the last ten in *The Rocking Chair and Other Poems* (1948). The texts are reprinted from the above sources.

Acknowledgements

We wish to thank the following authors, publishers and copyright holders for permission to reproduce the poems in this book.

BEHRMAN HOUSE INC.: for selection from *Hath not a Jew* by A. M. Klein, published by Behrman House Inc., 1261 Broadway, New York.

THE JEWISH PUBLICATION SOCIETY OF AMERICA: for selections from *Poems* by A. M. Klein reprinted by permission of the Jewish Publication Society of America.

THE MACMILLAN COMPANY OF CANADA LIMITED AND THE ESTATE OF E. J. PRATT: for selections from *The Collected Poems of E. J. Pratt*, reprinted by permission of the Estate of E. J. Pratt and The Macmillan Company of Canada Limited.

DOROTHY LIVESAY MACNAIR: for selections from *Green Pitcher, Signpost New Poems*, and *The Colour of God's Face*; and also for "Ballad of Me" originally published in *The Canadian Forum*.

NEW DIRECTIONS: for selection from *The Hitleriad* by A. M. Klein, Copyright 1944 by New Directions, reprinted by permission of the publishers, New Directions.

OXFORD UNIVERSITY PRESS: for selections from *Collected Poems* by by A. J. M. Smith by permission of Oxford University Press, Toronto.

THE RYERSON PRESS: for selections from *The Rocking Chair* by A. M. Klein and for selections from *Selected Poems* by Dorothy Livesay, reprinted by permission of The Ryerson Press, Toronto.

F. R. SCOTT: for selections from *Selected Poems*, published by Oxford University Press, reprinted by permission of the author.

SELECTED NEW CANADIAN LIBRARY TITLES

Asterisks (*) denote titles of New Canadian Library Classics

McCLELLAND & STEWART INC.,
publishers of The New Canadian Library,
would like to keep you informed about
new additions to this unique series.

For a complete listing of titles and
current prices – or if you wish to be added
to our mailing list to receive future catalogues
and other new book information – write:

BOOKNEWS
McClelland & Stewart Inc.
481 University Avenue
Toronto, Canada M5G 2E9

McClelland & Stewart books are
available at all good bookstores.

Booksellers should be happy to order from our catalogues
any titles which they do not regularly stock.